Elaine Rendler

In The Midst Of The Assembly

OCP Publications

We sincerely thank the various publishers who so generously allowed the reprinting of quotes in this volume. These publishers are listed in the Bibliography (p. 188-190).

Publisher: John Limb

Executive Editor: Bari Colombari *(with sincere thanks to D. & D.)*

Editorial Assistance: Geri Ethen, Tia Regan

Cover Art: Sheila Keefe of Alexandria, VA

Cover Design: Jean Germano, Ralph Sanders

Page Layout: Ralph Sanders

© 1994, OCP Publications, All rights reserved.
5536 N.E. Hassalo, Portland, OR 97213-3638
Printed in the United States of America

ISBN 0-915531-37-2

Contents

7. Rites and Sacraments

Introduction and Dedication

A few years ago (can you believe 1986?), John Limb, OCP's liturgy editor, now publisher of Oregon Catholic Press, had an idea about how OCP could be of help to parish musicians. He convinced Owen Alstott, who was publisher at the time, to enable him to reformat and expand a seasonal liturgy planner to be called *Today's Liturgy*. The purpose of *Today's Liturgy* would be twofold: to help the liturgical musician organize and prepare music for liturgy, and to help further the cause of liturgical renewal right out there in the midst of the action — in the parish. The focus would be pastoral, not academic. John then approached me to write a weekly column about music ministry and music preparation to share with musicians. I insisted that my medium was musical notes, not the written word, but to no avail. The columns were to be practical, pastoral, and, most of all, brief.

So we began. Copies were sent to every parish in the country. *Today's Liturgy* was certainly noticed. People who were involved in other liturgical ministries wrote and asked for information regarding their liturgical ministries as well. This included folks involved with liturgy committees, presiders, catechists, even pastors.

At first, I simply wrote my columns based on the scriptures of the given Sunday. As time moved on, readership grew and so did the role of *Today's Liturgy* readers in the liturgical life of the parish. They were getting involved with all kinds of liturgical celebration, preparation for sacraments, training of ministers, implementation of new rites and documents — even the building of new buildings. So the columns broadened to meet the needs of a fast-growing corps of liturgical ministers who were called to serve.

New challenges arose as time moved on. Longtime readers were hungry for new insights and creative ideas for ministry; new subscribers needed to know the basics. So, at the urging of John Limb and Bari Colombari, and all those workshop participants who wanted the columns put in book form, here it is.

For those who are just beginning liturgical ministry, here's a sampling of some of the columns that dealt with the basics of liturgy and ministry. For those of us who've been around a little longer, I hope that what's here is more than a memory of our years together.

Rather than weave the columns into long continuous chapters that attempt to cover every possible aspect of a subject, we decided to let them stay as short, specific items, organized around several general categories. I've tried to keep them brief and to the point so that none would require more than a few minutes of the free time I know you don't have. It's also a form that perhaps might be helpful for your bulletins or for ministry training.

You can be sure of one thing — these words are not based on theory, but on practical, hard-lived experience. May our shared experiences give us hope, and new experiences give us reason to keep on! And don't forget to keep laughing.

This book is dedicated to
all church musicians who
labor to prepare the feast.

Elaine Rendler
April, 1994

Part I

Who We Are

1
Our Call...

What It's Really All About

Let's begin by taking a few moments to reflect on our life and work in the Lord's vineyard. What exactly is the purpose of our liturgical ministry?

We hope that our ministry is a way of achieving our own salvation. We hope that it is also a way of helping others move toward the Lord.

We need to ask ourselves a question: Over the past year, have we become more loving people through our ministry? There are ministers who are so creative, talented, and resourceful that many people are drawn to them. They are natural leaders and usually have the support of a good number of people. In some cases, they wield much power because of their charisma. But, as St. Paul tells us, the true sign of a charism rooted in the Spirit is the amount of charity that is poured forth from a person or group.

With this last statement in mind, let's go back to our question: Have we become more loving people because of our particular ministry? And have we helped the people that we serve become more charitable toward one another? We are all familiar with the struggles of liturgical ministry — whether they revolve around music, rubrics, artwork, sacraments, or even plastic votive lights. These struggles will always be with us in some form. It is the way of life of a truly charismatic leader to put an end to that which divides our people — and to bring unity (not to be confused with conformity) to our people so that they too may become aware that there are many mansions in God's house.

Beware of tunnel vision in worship.

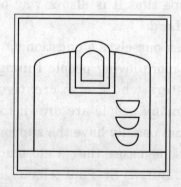

What's Involved in the Call

God calls us to service. Many of us have found that we are called to serve God primarily through the church and, in particular, the liturgy. We have an opportunity to be formed by the liturgy. We work regularly with liturgical prayers, texts, and music. Do we live by what we sing and profess? If we do, we become more loving people and we act in loving ways. But our parish work will not be holy work if it does not develop our potential to love and to become the best of that which we call human.

If we serve in the model of Jesus then we must be willing to become holy as Jesus did through prayer. We must be willing to listen as he did to the woman at the well. We must be willing to challenge as he challenged Peter and the disciples so many times, to shepherd as the Good Shepherd who lays down his life for his sheep, and to forgive seventy times seven. But all must be done out of love and with a selfless concern for the good of others.

What's the Cost of Answering the Call?

Father Walter J. Burghardt, SJ, says that the risen Christ destroyed distance by becoming present to devoted Magdalen, to Thomas, to two disciples en route to Emmaus, and to seven apostles at a seafood breakfast. But what about the risen Christian?

In *Still Proclaiming Your Wonders*, Father Burghardt writes:

> Here, gathered around the table on which the risen Christ will rest, here is a splendid spot to begin seeking things that are below. Here we minister to each other, awesomely aware that each of us is a wounded healer — risen indeed with Christ but still frightfully flawed, needing another's touch, another's "Peace!" In healing touch with one another, we can move out from these walls . . . not to Mother Teresa's Calcutta . . . but to the acres on which we dance so lightly. For me there are the red-brick buildings to my right that house 63 of my [Jesuit] brothers. Two of them died this winter: one's movement to death was tortuous, the other's unexpectedly swift. Where was I in their dying, where in their living? . . . [Amidst my world] what figure do I project? The self-righteous Pharisee or the compassionate Christ? Or . . . just nothing?

Father Burghardt then uses Sydney Carter's text, "Lord of the Dance" ("I danced in the morning"), and ends with these thoughts: It is a "risk-laden dance, this risen dance; for it opens your dance card to all manner of dancers; some of them will dance on your toes. But it has the built-in joy no man or woman can take from you, if . . . if you let the Lord of the Dance 'lead you wherever you may be.'"

You may want to read this text at a rehearsal or meeting. Or perhaps quote it in your bulletin.

A Good Music Program . . .

What do we mean when we say that a parish has a really good music program? Does it mean that the choir sounds wonderful? That brass is hired for special occasions? That the people sing well? That even if the people don't sing, the music is beautiful?

Frankly, there wouldn't be enough space in this entire book to define what is meant by good musical liturgy. Everyone has an opinion. Some say the quality of the music must be great regardless of the abilities of the assembly. Others say we need to challenge the assembly. Others don't give a hoot about the assembly as long as they can perform the works of the great masters (only the best is good enough for God). Much of the discussion centers on the musical tastes of the ministers. Some of it is rooted in the musician's own theology.

I am sure of these few things about this subject:

· For worship we must have a solid body of music that includes more than hymns.

· We need acclamations, psalms, music for the rites, and texts that express the theology of Vatican II.

· We must tell our whole story in song, not just sing the songs of a particular era or style.

· We must stop giving people texts with weak theology no matter how much we like the music.

· We need a marriage of text and tune — musically and theologically.

· We must extend the musical prayer of the parish beyond solely devotional music.

· We must hold on to the best from the past, grieve the losses, and then move on to create new music for worship.

Artists and Servants . . .

[T]o paint a picture or to write a story or to compose a song is an incarnational activity. The artist is a servant who is willing to be a birthgiver. In a very real sense the artist (male or female) should be like Mary who, when the angel told her that she was to bear the Messiah, was obedient to the command.

Obedience is an unpopular word nowadays, but the artist must be obedient to the work, whether it be a symphony, a painting, or a story for a small child. I believe that each work of art, whether it is a work of great genius, or something very small, comes to the artist and says, "Here I am. Enflesh me. Give birth to me." And the artist either says, "My soul doth magnify the Lord," and willingly becomes the bearer of the work, or refuses; but the obedient response is not necessarily a conscious one, and not everyone has the humble, courageous obedience of Mary.

— Madeleine L'Engle

(Reprinted from *Walking on Water: Reflections on Faith and Art,* by Madeleine L'Engle, © 1980 by Crosswicks. Used by permission of Harold Shaw Publishers, Wheaton, IL.)

Each week we artists are called to enflesh a musical liturgy, to be obedient servants to the liturgy and creative bearers of the "work." We are not drones who restate "the theme" in musical notes, nor are we to "do our own thing." Magnify the Lord, and reflect on the themes of the season or feast that permeate our lives: God becomes one of us, and, just as important, we become part of the divine.

Dear Creator . . .

The word "artist" is almost synonymous with the word "creative." In the creative process, we come close to an understanding of the One who made us all, whose first title is CREATOR. Let us give thanks with excerpts from Ted Loder's poem, "I Claim Your Power To Create."

O Ingenious One, it is not only creation,
But creativity that awes me.
It is a wondrous thing
That you share your power to create.

O Mysterious One, I shrink from your power,
Yet I claim it;
And it is mine by Your genius or madness,
This power to speak and have light burst upon a mind,
Or darkness descend upon a heart;
This power to make music to which souls dance
or armies march;
This power to mold and paint and carve
And so spin out the stars
By which I plot my course to heaven or to hell . . .

O Daring One, it is an awesome power you've shared;
And I rejoice in the artists
Who dare to use their gift
To create the beauty which casts this world
Into a more whole and holy dimension,
Who dare to breathe visions and vibrations into dullness,
As You breathed life into dust.

Preparing a Feast . . .
Generation to Generation

My favorite part of traveling is meeting you. You're worth the endless packing and repacking of suitcases, bumpy airplane landings, and hours of airport waiting. Your level of commitment, faith, and generosity is awesome. You care about the people of God and the liturgy of the church. Your excellent service and sometimes heroic ministry deserve notice.

While giving a liturgical ministry workshop weekend at Blessed Sacrament Parish in Valley Stream, N.Y., I heard Father Greg Cappuccino preach a great homily that gave us all a "shot in the arm." He described eucharistic ministers, readers, hospitality ministers, music ministers, and preachers as called to work in God's kitchen.

Do you love it? Here we are, asked to prepare a feast. Everyone does something: plans menus, cooks food, sweeps floors, taste-tests, polishes silver, chooses china, arranges flowers, and rehearses the band. (Yes, this is a special kitchen with a rehearsal area for the band.) I like the image of preparing a feast much more than that of laboring in a vineyard. I prefer preparing parties to picking grapes. How about you?

Do you know what scares me, though? I don't see many apprentices coming along. Have you noticed that, too?

We music ministers work here together preparing this feast because someone invited us into the "kitchen." If you are a music minister, you know how important it is to invite a child early on to become a music minister. It takes a long time and a lot of work to become a good musician. The church has a tradition of beautiful music, passed from generation to generation. But who will make music for the next generation? Music is losing its place in the school curriculum these days. And the "music nuns" are rare now. So who will teach our great choral music to the children that they might sing it and cherish it and feed their souls with it? If ever there was a time to attend to and nurture children's choirs, that time is now.

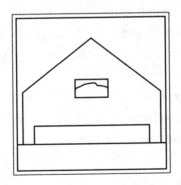

The Cost of Commitment

All across the country we musicians and liturgy planners try faithfully to use our gifts for the building of the kingdom. It's not easy. Those for whom this ministry is a life-giving vocation suffer much to be faithful to it. I heard a story of a musician who had to move out of her office so that old file cabinets could be stored in there, and of a pastor whose entire choir walked out because he asked them to sing facing the assembly. I know a fine pastoral musician who has been asked not to sing because his voice is "too beautiful." I know priests who have to go away to recuperate from exhaustion because of the priest shortage. No, it's not easy. And it's not getting any easier.

On the other hand, there's a lot of good news. Some folks tell me they love their parish, their pastor, their people, their musicians. Choirs that consisted of only two or three persons five years ago are full of life, energy, and more members today. More and more musicians are being paid a decent salary. Musicians tell me that finally, after all these years, "Father" understands what they're saying. (Perhaps the musician is speaking more clearly.)

And so it goes. Ups and downs . . . but never boring. Let's take a moment to reflect on the good things that continue to happen. We have much to be thankful for: life, breath, music, health, community, church, musicians, and love. We've got running water and nobody's shooting at us when we wake up. That's more than a lot of people on this planet can say. Don't let a day pass without looking for that "good thing."

Pledges of Allegiance

Here are a few resolutions on commitment for those in music ministry. These may be adapted for other ministries.

1. I have been called to serve God's people through my music. As a responsible caretaker of this gift, I will set aside quality time in my life to prepare my music and to become familiar with the prayers and readings of the liturgies at which I serve.

2. Even though I may think my gift is small, I will remember that the greatest return I can make to the Lord is to develop and increase my gift and share it with others.

3. I will put the needs of the worshiping community ahead of my personal desires and avoid using this ministry to meet my own needs, musically or otherwise.

4. I will try to live in conformity with what I sing and proclaim.

5. I will minister in the model of Jesus who always loved those he served.

Keep the Faith, Baby

In recent years I have been privileged to meet many of you musicians. Not only are you talented, but your perseverance and patience are inspirational. The dedication and commitment with which you serve your people humbles me. Why? For several reasons. It's not because, as a musician, I know just how much behind-the-scenes work is involved in preparing a music program for a parish. Nor because I, too, know the pain and privilege of working collaboratively. Nor is it because I am aware of the dying to one's ideas that is sometimes required of all of us who minister. I am humbled by you because most of you respond as do the servants in Luke's gospel (17:5–10): "We have done no more than our duty."

The sentence just before that one reads, "We are useless servants." If this quote hits you in the face, be sure to read the whole passage. You only need faith the size of a mustard seed to command a sycamore tree to be uprooted and transplanted into the sea. If you didn't have faith, you wouldn't even care to serve in ministry. And whether or not you realize it, you have moved more than one sycamore tree into the sea . . . several times over.

If you sometimes feel discouraged, perhaps it's not because you don't have faith, but because you don't feel successful. But what is success to a Christian? The cross is always before us and the vision is worth dying for. Habakkuk gives us encouragement: "For the vision still has its time, presses on to fulfillment, and will not disappoint; if it delays, wait for it, it will surely come, it will not be late" (2:3). Lord, increase our faith and sustain our vision!

Our Challenge

Let's face it. Our church is being pushed and pulled in many directions. Many wonder where things are going. What will happen? Where will we go? . . . Some things never change. The poor are still poor, and the hungry still go hungry.

In Mark 6:30–34, we hear: " . . . Jesus saw a vast crowd. He pitied them, for they were like sheep without a shepherd; and he began to teach them at great length." Monika Hellwig, in *Gladness Their Escort*, suggests that "there is great depth of meaning in the apparently casual remark of the evangelist Mark that Jesus had compassion for the crowds that clung to him in times when he needed some solitude and quiet, because Jesus saw that they were like sheep without a shepherd. It implies the vocation to gather and guide, to show the way and offer a sense of purpose and a reason for hope."

After a particularly discouraging day in the trenches of ministry, I ran into a priest friend from the Raleigh, North Carolina diocese who works in liturgy. I asked him how he could smile in the midst of all this messiness. "Because I have hope," he replied. "We must be persons of hope for each other. If we're not, why be involved in ministry, anyway?"

Be persons of hope for everyone you meet, whether it be at a communion station, a hospital bed, an ambo, the classroom, the office, the marketplace. Be a good leader. Show the way. Offer those you serve a sense of purpose and a reason for hope.

Our Struggles

According to Luke (4:24), "no prophet is accepted in the prophet's hometown." At least you have scriptural sources in which to take refuge.

On the subject of unpopularity, please note: Losing a job in ministry does not mean personal failure. All of us in this vocation have had to move on at one time or another. There can be many reasons for this. Probably the most common is a change of administration within the parish structure. (This is known in the vernacular as getting a new pastor.) Perhaps the vision is different now, or the personalities don't work. It is not uncommon in this country for a new president to appoint a new cabinet to help promote a "new vision" for the country. God bless America.

But there are other reasons why a musician might end up looking for a new parish. Sometimes the musician is the instrument of renewal (commonly known among friends as the agitating force) in a parish. If the musician pushes too quickly for change, or tries to implement change without adequate catechesis for the assembly or committee members, division occurs, wounds are inflicted, and the musician takes the rap (no pun intended). Changes, even necessary ones, are painful — especially at church, where some people would like to think that nothing ever changes.

And growth is painful, too. If your parish is unwilling to grow, and you represent the instrument of growth, you may find yourself looking for a new job. But this doesn't mean you have failed. Perhaps it was your task to plant the seeds. You have planted the seeds so that your successor may reap. Sometimes the ground may have to lie fallow. But there will be a harvest.

Care of Ourselves

Be good to yourself. Remember, when we become as involved with the implementation of Sunday liturgy as many of us are, we run the risk of becoming mundane about our work, of losing the sense of the mystery of Christ's redeeming action in the liturgy. Musicians know exactly what I'm talking about. It's no easy trick trying to manage a music group, and possibly an instrument, while being present to the action of the liturgy and our own prayer. Musicians and ministers who serve at multiple liturgies on a weekend can be especially susceptible. Why? Because we must put so much energy into each liturgy that we are exhausted and sometimes running on automatic pilot by the last Mass. I am not suggesting that there is a solution to this problem, but it might be a good idea to take some time out once in a while to reflect on the mystery in which we are privileged to have a share.

We must not lose sight of the greatness and the holiness of the work to which we are called. No liturgy is ordinary. No liturgy is without mystery. Do you ever ask yourself why people keep coming back Sunday after Sunday? There is a profound mystery at the heart of our Sunday worship that we can never fully understand but which is central to the lives of people. To paraphrase Father Austin Fleming in *Yours Is a Share:* What we do at liturgy is holy. Through it we become holy.

How Far
How Fast . . .

Just because parish celebrations fall short of our professional expectations doesn't mean that there is no improvement in the quality of worship or its impact on people's lives. Don't underestimate how influential we are or what a difference we can make. Changes that may seem minute to us are sometimes very substantial in the eyes of the people. Always consider how *far* the parish has come . . . not how *fast*.

Remember: Part of ministry is to teach. But being a good teacher doesn't mean you have to show people how knowledgeable you are. A good teacher is tuned in to what the students are capable of learning and at what pace. Put egos aside and walk with your people as they journey.

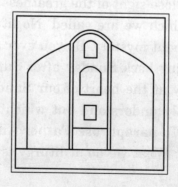

Musical Training

Music can truly be a source of joy, conversion, comfort, and healing in our liturgies. By its very nature, assembly singing is a community experience. Music can be a doorway to the holy. It expresses the inexpressible. It can reveal the transcendent to the human spirit. It can help people learn and remember texts and prayers. It can teach doctrine and religious principles. It has the potential to communicate deeply to the heart.

For any or all of the above to happen, however, musical training is required. Effective music in worship demands trained musical leadership. It is not true that musical training involves only the pursuit of aesthetic goals. But it is true that aesthetics, or beauty, is an intrinsic part of the ministry of music. In music ministry the most basic form of beauty is the sound of the assembly's singing. To achieve this kind of beauty one needs musical, not liturgical, skill.

The ministry of music is still a downright exciting field. The conditions may not be the greatest, and congregations are still more apt to pay for "things" than for services, but the work itself? It just doesn't get much better than this, folks! Music is not just an art form; it is an instrument of the Holy Spirit. It is a ministry of the gospel.

Learn Your Craft

Some musicians have written to me about the difficulty of working with small parishes that don't have a lot of resources. What do you do when there are only a few musicians to help out? What do you do when you don't have much music background and accept the ministry because there's no one else who can do it? How do you start a choir? What about repertoire for small choirs? There are so many questions!

Well, the first thing to do is decide if you feel called to this ministry. Then discern whether or not the community has called you to it. If you are in a parish where you have been named "musician," then accept it. Some of you may think you're inadequate because you don't have a degree in music. Not necessarily true. Some of you may feel inadequate because you can't read music. Now there's a real problem! But this is a problem of literacy, not necessarily of gift. If you don't read music, then learn. With all the innovations of modern technology you can learn the science of note reading and play a basic keyboard. I realize that resources may be limited, but I strongly encourage you to learn your craft as much as possible. The question is not how much you know today, but how you can return your gift to the Lord.

I think you'll be surprised how much better you'll feel about your ministry if you develop your craft. It's never too late to start. Remember Grandma Moses!

I Can Never Reach You in Your Office

Let's focus on just three words from Mark's gospel (4:39): "Quiet! Be Still!" Musicians especially need to take some time out for themselves lest they face the occupational hazard known as burnout. There are several causes of burnout. Here are a few thoughts on two of them.

It's 11 P.M. Why is the light still on in the music office?

The first cause of burnout revolves around the amount of time (not to mention the odd hours) and kind of energy involved in music ministry. Much more is involved than meets the eye (particularly the assembly's). Besides planning and meetings, rehearsals and preparation for rehearsals, there are also the daily tasks of practicing one's instrument or voice, keeping abreast of a constantly developing and changing area of ministry, and being present to the lives of the people in our communities. Many of our clergy wrestle with this struggle, but only some of them notice the similarities to music ministry. Only another musician can truly identify with the difficulties and complexities of a life in pastoral music.

Gosh, I seem to be getting a cold again.

The second reason for burnout piggybacks on the first. Because music ministry tends to be seasonal, musicians find themselves extremely involved and stressed during busy liturgical seasons. Adrenaline flows steadily during the intense days before a feast; and then, immediately after, musicians collapse for a few days in order to recuperate. This kind of lifestyle is unhealthy — not only for the individual, but also for the community. Why? Because communities need healthy and inspirational leaders in music ministry. If you don't take care of yourself and take time to relax and replenish, you might just decide to throw in the towel — and WE NEED YOU! Avoid messianic tendencies. Don't confuse working in the Lord's vineyard with owning the vineyard! TAKE A BREAK!

Dear Father . . .

A word about clergy/musician relationships:

Dear Father,

We musicians know that we are one of the most visible ministries in the parish. We also know that we affect practically every member of the parish who attends liturgy. If we don't affect them, we aren't doing our job. Some will like what we do, others won't. And we understand that, more often than not, people will come to you with their complaints rather than their praises for the music. In fact, that probably holds true for most ministries in the parish. But, if we are to fashion a people, part of our job is to stretch people's minds, affect their senses, and knock at the door of their hopes and fears. And we rejoice in that. We also realize that we are only one ministry. When there's a complaint in youth ministry it comes to you. When someone's not happy with what's going on in religious education, they come to you. When there's financial trouble, they come to you. Even when the pipes are leaking, you'll probably be the first to know. When the bishop gets a complaint letter from one of the parishioners, he doesn't notify your staff members or a committee, he notifies *you*.

Please help us to do our job. We expect people to react to our music. We are trained to handle that. It is our ministry. What we need you to do is to support us by telling the complainer to bring any music complaint directly to us. There's more to life than complaining about church music. Something deeper is usually going on. At least give us a chance to encounter the person and to minister to what the problem really is.

It takes a lot of courage for you to back us, especially if the complainer is an important parishioner. But even the most savvy CEO would agree that it's important to back the staff. You don't have to keep getting caught in the middle. Let's help each other. After all, it's the Christian way.

Sincerely,
The Musicians

Ministry: A Definition

Let us reflect on these words from Fr. William Bauman's *The Ministry of Music* (second edition).

Ministry is service rendered out of love, and with a deep respect for the person served, after the model of Jesus. Ministry is never self-seeking; ministry is giving, and it is the kind of giving in which one loves the persons one gives to. To bring joy, to bring relief from pain and sorrow, to end anxiety and fear, to share what enriches — this is ministry. Ministry is not an attempt to do someone over in some preconceived pattern. It uncritically respects the individuality, taste, and life choices of the persons served, freeing them to create themselves anew. It urges, inspires, shares, supports; it never forces.

Bauman's words continue to remind me of who I am and who I want to become.

2

Ministry, Recruitment, and Hospitality

New Members — Is There Enough Room?

Do we ministers serve in the model of Jesus when it comes to being open to new members in music groups or committees? Are we open to people who might not "fit in" simply because they are different from what we're used to? Does our ministry of hospitality include the gifted — including gifted women? Do we reject people whose ideas or personalities are different from ours? Are we willing to let go of our own ideas (not ideals) with the trust that someone else's ideas may be different yet valid? Are we fearful of losing our place as the "creative" person to someone else?

One of the more difficult gospel challenges is to be open to the stranger. Do we save a seat in church for someone we know rather than trying to get to know someone new? Or might we tell a person that the music group has no openings?

I am in no way suggesting that persons who lack the appropriate gifts be accepted into a ministry that requires a specific talent or skill. But we must not refuse talented people a chance to use their gifts simply because they won't "fit in." It may be *our* fault, not theirs, that they don't fit in. And many times it is our loss that we are not open enough to celebrate the difference. How beautiful is the bouquet of many kinds of flowers!

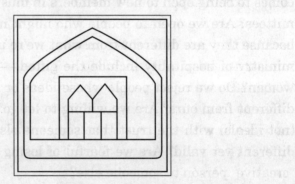

Commitment Is the Response

In music ministry, commitment is as essential as a good voice — a good voice is the call, commitment is the response. When we allow a half-committed volunteer to sing, we set ourselves up for disappointment and eventually become annoyed with the new musician. This situation can be destructive both to the music group and to the new member. (This is true for all other liturgical ministries as well.) Be up front with volunteers. Tell them exactly what's expected before they make their commitment. Trust me. They'll take their commitment more seriously if you're serious about it.

Just as a catechumen comes to us to "try out" our parish communities, music ministers want a chance to find out what the group is like and to see how things work before making a commitment. Liturgical ministries are not simply tasks to be performed. Music ministry is a way of life, a way of living in the world. Ask any church musician.

Recruitment

When Jesus called forth Peter, Andrew, James, and John to follow him, it didn't take much convincing. They agreed to follow almost immediately. Wouldn't it be nice if we could recruit liturgical ministers so easily?

But don't be hasty making a pitch for liturgical ministers. We need to help people discern their gifts before we ask them to fill a ministerial position. This pertains even to volunteers. A few good readers will be better than a dozen readers who don't communicate well. For musicians, discernment is accomplished through an audition. For other ministers, an interview is essential. It is time that we recognize quality as well as quantity.

Recruitment Begins with Registering New Parishioners

Today's society is quite transient compared to that of a generation ago. It's not like the days of Dobie Gillis and the Beaver when life revolved around the neighborhood. People are moving from place to place more frequently than ever before. If your parish is alive and well you will be attracting new members regularly. How does your parish handle the registration of new parishioners? Do you remember how it used to be done? I'm afraid the old model is still more prevalent than one would suspect.

For those of you too young to remember, in the past people who wanted to join the parish simply knocked on the rectory door and told the secretary they wished to "register." Several required forms would be filled out — forms with questions pertaining to mixed marriages and the state of grace of the kids. Whatever. One of the most important questions was where to send the church envelopes. Golly, gee, aren't we glad those days are over? Oops.

On the other hand, when recruitment season rolls around, practically every committee in the parish is out recruiting new members. There are notices in the bulletin. There are pleas in the announcements for volunteers for just about everything under the sun. There are card tables outside the church to sign up for events, and probably there are cards in the pews to be filled out. And you can bet your life that we music directors are out there with the best of them.

Why am I talking about registration and recruitment? Because registration, if done properly, will yield an abundance of volunteers. Instead of simply handing folks a form, why not begin by welcoming them and taking the time to chat with them and show them around? Begin to build a relationship. In some parishes, new members are invited to a group orientation. A more personal approach effectively builds communities as well as ministries. Ask about the occupations, hobbies, skills, and talents of new parishioners. In what activities did they participate in their previous parish? How would they like to serve in this parish? Some people don't want to serve at all. (They just might need a rest from the last parish.) Others are just waiting to be asked. Relationship cultivates a sense of belonging and ownership. Try it.

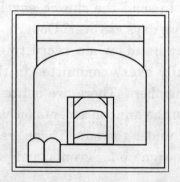

Techniques for Ministry Recruitment

When we take for granted the process by which new members enter the parish, we let many talented people slip through our fingers — people who might otherwise enrich both themselves and our community. Then we must go about the business of seeking volunteers through the church bulletin, which we all know is read by only a very few. But, you say, don't forget that there are always pulpit announcements.

While we're on the subject of pulpit announcements and recruitment, let me say that they don't produce many positive results. This goes twice for recruiting people for music ministry. There is, however, a method that has proven effective. Let the music minister make a brief presentation to the assembly about the music ministry just after the other announcements at Masses on a particular Sunday.

It's really important that music ministers themselves make the pitch. When I do it, I never say that we *need* anyone. I offer people the opportunity to grow in their faith and become part of one terrific community within the parish — the music community. Why do I say it that way? Because it's the truth. The musicians do make up a wonderful community, and we all grow with the experience. I also tell them that we will be taking in new "recruits" for the next month. They're more than welcome to try us out for a few weeks before deciding. (It almost sounds as serious as joining the catechumenate. Well, it is, almost.)

Finally, I tell the assembly that if they are interested in this ministry please see me immediately after Mass over at the piano. Strike while the iron is hot! I don't think it's a good idea to tell people to call you at the office, to look in the bulletin for details, or to just come to the next rehearsal. I think it's really important to talk personally to the interested parties, to initiate the relationship, to make them feel welcome and comfortable.

Pastors and committees who understand the importance of good preaching and good music at liturgy will be willing to give time for this music ministry "commercial." The commercial should only take place once or twice a year, and it should certainly last no longer than three to four minutes.

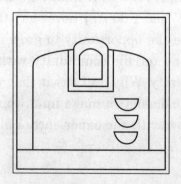

Recruitment: The Ultimate Test

Do you find it hard to recruit people for your music ministry? If the choir is hurting for members, what's the real problem? Before you blame the pastor, the parishioners, the base/foot/basketball season, or the weather, consider putting together a choir recruitment "kit" like the one I find useful.

First, you will need some ordinary technology that every successful recruiter already has: either an audio or a video recorder. Tape your music group several times — not just on special feasts: I'm talking Sundays in Ordinary Time.

If you want people to serve with all their skill and grace, then your group had better sound decent. Tapes tell the truth. Who's the judge of that? Not members of the group. Ask other musicians.

Now for the director: If you pass the tape test, then how about the mirror test? You — what have you done to recruit people? Does the assembly know you? Do you get up on your own to recruit new members through announcements? Or do you weasel out of it by asking the lector to do it? Sorry. That won't work as well. If you're too shy (oh, please!) or not a good speaker, let another music minister do it. Look for a prepared, outgoing, fun person to make the case. Keep it short and energetic. And none of that pious talk about how people should really *want* to serve if they have musical gifts (what sane humans care to make a God-given talent sound like a God-awful joke?).

How We See Ourselves (and Others)

Both the Hebrew and Christian testaments warn us about clericalism. Lay ministers will be the first to object to any clericalism among the clergy. But what about clericalism among the laity? Several stories come to mind.

The first story: the blessing of the throats after Sunday liturgy. Who did it? Good news: the priests *and* the laity. But who? The eucharistic ministers. Why them? Nothing against eucharistic ministers, but why not use people who are involved in the healing professions, such as doctors, nurses, and hospital workers? After all, this ministry is what they are about in their professional lives, and probably in their personal lives as well.

The second story: Ash Wednesday. Distribution of ashes. Who did it? Good news: laity and ordained were distributing. A woman approached her friend afterward and asked, "Why are you giving out ashes? You're not a eucharistic minister."

The third story: Sunday morning, 2050. Father is ill and cannot celebrate Mass this Sunday. Who will preside at the communion service? What ministry would you look to first to find a presider for the communion service? Eucharistic ministers? Why?

I bring this up not to bash eucharistic ministers but to raise the issue of clericalism among the laity. Are eucharistic ministers regarded as more important than other specialized liturgical ministers? Does the laity have a hierarchy based on the minister's proximity to the eucharistic table and the sanctuary? The question is not who is the rightful heir when the priest cannot be there, but who can best do the job. The community will name that person if you ask. Try this with your committees. It works. But the choice may surprise you (especially if you think that *you're* the rightful heir).

Celebrity or Service?

"Whoever wants to be first, must be last of all and servant of all" (Mark 9:35). Lest we give only lip service to these words, let's look at our liturgical practice to make sure we practice what we preach.

Place yourself in the pew for a moment. We tell ourselves and our assemblies that the assembly is the primary celebrator of liturgy.

Now . . .

Are the eucharistic ministers part of the entrance procession? If so, for what purpose? Does it make them special? Why aren't they seated with you as assembly members until it's time for them to serve? Will they fuss if they are taken out of the procession? (If so, perhaps they need some re-evaluation of their role and the function of processions.)

What are we saying to the people in the pews when all the ministers receive eucharist first? I know there are good reasons for doing this, but should the assembly members sit and watch the ministers (servants) eat first? Is this how we treat guests? This unspoken message — that the ministers are more important than the assembly — gets even louder when the musicians also receive first, because there is usually dead silence while everyone watches the "special people" being served.

What is communicated to the assembly when musicians say, "Please join us in our opening hymn"? Who is *us*? The ministers? The musicians? Wouldn't it be more appropriate to say, "Our opening hymn is . . ."? Wouldn't this kind of invitation be more inclusive of the persons in the pews?

Oh, yes — one more thing. Can we get away from announcing the names of those who perform specialized ministries? Perhaps name tags or badges for ministers would be a better solution. We're trying to get the assembly to participate and understand that they are the most important celebrators of the liturgy. Do we treat them like observers or the most important guests? Does anyone ask their names as well?

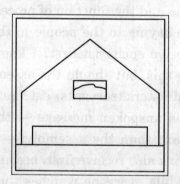

We Are the Church

For years the church was viewed by many as an authoritarian institution with its authority vested solely in the hierarchy. More emphasis was placed on ordination than on baptism. The clergy were the "doers" and the laity became "do-ees." Lay ministry, where it existed, was seen as a way of assisting the clergy.

When asked today who the church is, the first response is usually that it is the people of God. Today's church follows a model that calls for much more than one small group of people ministering to others ("doers and do-ees"). To be church demands that the local parish be more than a "spiritual filling station" for its members. A church community must be more than people coming together for worship on Sunday and then going their separate ways until next time. The New Testament calls us to a shared life together in Jesus Christ. But how can we share life together if we don't know one another? We are called to use our gifts for the good of the community. But how can we do this unless we know the community's needs?

Hospitality

Begin with hospitality. Hospitality, you say? Such a word! Outdated? Ever heard it used in church during your "wonder years"? No one ever used it in any of my theology classes in college — how about yours? Personally, I've always connected hospitality with social graces and hotel services. You know what I mean: clean towels, a chocolate on the pillow, free coffee in the lobby, and "We'll leave the light on for ya!" So what do we mean when we talk about hospitality in church? Free coffee in the vestibule?

Although hospitality evokes a variety of meanings, at Sunday worship it has a particular meaning. It means going out of one's way to help others, to make them feel welcome, to let strangers know they belong. It means the beginning of relationship. Jesus always welcomed those who were his own. We welcome others because Christ did. It is one way that Christ becomes enfleshed and visible in the Christian assembly. This is the work of the people of God. It is a call from our baptism.

Liturgy is the source and font of our parish life. It is not an end in itself. It is our human way of getting in touch with who we are in relation to God and one another. Yes, the liturgy should be done well. But it must be more than just a "good show." As long as the poor are hungry in our parishes (and it's going to get worse), as long as persons with disabilities have no access, as long as the stranger in our midst is unwelcome, as long as there are unhealthy or unchristian attitudes in our hearts, then we are merely paying lip service to our God. It is not the task of just the social justice committee to deal with these things; it is the task of all.

"Oh Mein PaPa..."

I took my father to Mass on a very cold Saturday evening. He doesn't get to go to church very often because he is a stroke patient who cannot walk or talk anymore. Just getting from home to church involves braces, arm slings, clothing assistance, transferring from wheelchair into car, collapsing a wheelchair and flinging it, as well as its accoutrements (seat and pillows), into the rear of a station wagon. The whole procedure continues when we reach the church, and then reverses when we come home (as many of you know from your own experiences).

So, we arrive at the church parking lot where there is one handicap parking space in sight. There's no extra space on either side of it for wheelchair access. Darn! I figure I'll pull up to the front door of the church, unload my dad, and then park the car. Darn! You guessed it. Into the handicap parking space zips a guy in his forties late for Mass. He has no handicap license plates. He's running into church. Right past us! 'Cause he's late for Mass. "Excuse me," I say in desperation, "can you tell me where there's other handicap parking?" "I have no idea," he responds defensively. Then he realizes he is caught.

Why? Differently-abled people and their caretakers know where handicap parking spaces are. Families with a member who uses a wheelchair are aware of things that never occur to the able bodied. They know where the elevators are in department stores. They know which shopping malls have handicap access, which motels and hotels are equipped for persons with disabilities (this means more than a safety railing in the bathtub), and where to go to a church that has alternatives to the steep front stairway. And they are always compassionate and hospitable to one another.

Later, from the rear of the church (there was no special seating), I saw the man in the communion procession. After we were all sent forth to love and serve the Lord, he and his seemingly able wife walked past us to their car while we began our pilgrimage in the cold night air to a distant parking space. Now, what's wrong with this picture?

I'm a fanatic about this, obviously. But this is no isolated incident. I know of one bride who decided not to get married in her home parish because there was no access into the church for her brother, who used a wheelchair. Actually, the final blow came when the pastor told her he would not allow a wheelchair in the sanctuary.

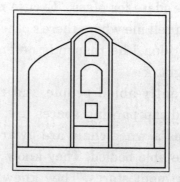

"All God's Chillun Got a Place . . ."

And there is my niece, Christen. When she was 18 months old, Christen was in an accident that left her severely brain damaged. As a result, she crossed over into the world of the differently abled.

Christen's family knows the embarrassment and anger of being asked to move her and her wheelchair from a church aisle because she was "in the way," although there was no area in the worship space to accommodate her except next to the rear door. But they also know the joy of acceptance by ministers who offer to help when they see her coming, who greet her and speak to her even though she cannot voice her response. They are also comforted by those Christian communities who by their actions show her young siblings that there's a place you can go where it's perfectly okay to have a sister who's "different." Indeed, there are parishes who not only appreciate, but *celebrate* the witness of the differently abled. They provide handicap access into the church — and into the sanctuary area as well — so that these people might serve as eucharistic ministers, lectors, etc.

The law demands handicap access ramps into public buildings, but apparently churches are exempt from this law. Now, I'm not so naive as to ignore the financial implications of this endeavor. It can be outrageously expensive. We clear spaces for music areas in our buildings — can't we clear some space for our brothers and sisters with special needs? This doesn't necessarily mean the front row. Why not consult with the differently abled about their needs? But keep in mind that they and their families are just as hungry, maybe even more so, to hear the Good News and share eucharist.

Sunday Mass should be a place where we can experience a foreshadowing of the heavenly banquet. It must be a place where everyone who enters is welcomed and made to feel worthy, accepted, and loved by all in the model of Jesus Christ, the host of the heavenly banquet. In my book, a parish that accepts differently-abled but capable people as cross bearers, lectors, eucharistic ministers, and so forth, is first class.

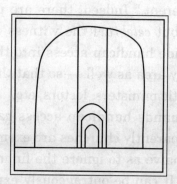

Hints for the Seemingly Abled

A few suggestions for attending to the needs of the differently abled:

1. If your parish is creating handicap parking, leave enough space for getting in and out of vehicles with equipment.

2. Follow specifications for building ramps. If yours resemble ski slopes, they're probably not up to code. Pray you'll never need to use them.

3. The politically correct term at the moment is "differently abled."

4. Some differently-abled people need special seating inside the church.

5. Just because people cannot speak doesn't mean they are stupid.

6. People who are developmentally delayed (for example, with mental retardation) have feelings.

7. When possible, direct conversation to the challenged person, not just to the caregiver.

3
Liturgical Ministers

Minister of Music — What Are the Ingredients?

People are singing more and more, and the quality of the music and texts is certainly improving. But the quality of the pastoral musician's own musicianship is still our primary concern. I have heard plenty of complaints about arrogant choir directors and snooty organists. I agree that a person must be more than a good choral director to be a good minister of music. I agree that there are organists who can play all the major works of Bach and still don't have a sense for good liturgy. But, in fact, the opposite is also true.

No one can be a good minister of music if he or she is not a good musician. I am weary of musicians who know facts better than musical notes. Some persons can quote *Music In Catholic Worship* until the cows come home, but it won't help one bit if their music group sounds bad. If a cantor doesn't understand how to relate to an assembly, he or she doesn't lack liturgical skills, but fundamental performance skills that are essential to the ministry of music. Do I sound a bit vehement about this? You bet I am.

Unless we musicians take our own work seriously, no one else will. Perhaps we need to invite some other musicians in the neighborhood to evaluate our liturgies from a musical standpoint. We will always be subject to the taste judgments of consumers; but are we willing to face an evaluation by our peers?

Teaching a New Song

Does teaching a new song to the assembly before Mass make you nervous? I used to dread it. It was always the scariest part of my role as leader of music. But now I'm used to it and so is the assembly.

Part of the problem is the physical arrangement of the worship space and the kind of expectations it sets up between the minister and assembly. Many of our worship spaces resemble concert halls. The liturgical action takes place up front, and the assembly sits in rows. Because of this, when I had to go to the microphone to speak, I felt like a performer before an audience. Looming in the recesses of my mind were nightmares of having to perform in student piano recitals while growing up.

What helped me was to re-image my role. I am not an entertainer when I'm preparing the assembly for worship. The experience need not be unpleasant for them, but I'm not there to entertain them, either. I don't tell jokes or perform for them. When I teach a song before Mass, my role is that of *teacher*. Once I claimed my role as teacher, I became comfortable with my task, and my self-confidence increased.

Many of us musicians have been trained as music educators. I have met excellent music teachers who suddenly become apologetic and shy in front of assemblies. If you think of yourself standing in front of a classroom instead of an audience, you may find yourself much more calm and effective in your ministry to the assembly.

To Sing or Not to Sing?

Learning to be flexible is one of the big challenges in liturgical ministry — music ministry in particular. It's crucial for us to know the notes well so that we are not tied to the page and are thus able to focus our attention on the music's message and the assembly's participation. At the same time, it's equally important that we be present to the movement of the Spirit and to what's happening at each moment of the celebration.

One of the charisms of a good liturgical minister is to go with the flow. Sometimes that means making last-minute changes — for example, surrendering a piece of music that we have prepared but that would be inappropriate in the context of the rhythmic flow of the celebration as it unfolds.

There is no place for rigidity in liturgical planning. Those who need to know everything that's going to happen and have their music so thoroughly rehearsed that they cannot move in any direction except that which is programmed, put themselves under stress and ultimately serve their own purpose and not that of the liturgy.

Remember: To prepare all the verses of a piece of music is part of the responsibility of the call to serve through music. In addition, not to use all the verses when they interfere with the movement of the ritual is also part of our call. Sometimes, to serve means *not* to sing!

Not Just the Facts, Ma'am

Nearly thirty years have passed since the end of the Second Vatican Council, and the music in our churches still varies from awful to tolerable to inspiring. I suspect that those places where music is described as "awful" suffer from a lack of craftsmanship on the part of the musician. More often than not, wrong notes are only one part of the problem — they're usually accompanied with "bad" tempos. The musician's heart might be in the right place — it's the heartbeat and fingers that are in question here.

In the final analysis, parishes must face this truth: The quality of the music program is absolutely dependent on the quality of the musician. Musical, liturgical, and pastoral information all contribute to the making of a pastoral musician. But the basic, primary question is: How musically skilled is the musician? The inability to lead or accompany assembly music will seriously affect the quality of community worship and can result in the destruction of a common worship experience for the assembly.

Hiring the Music Minister — What to Look For

". . . those who want to save their life will lose it, and those who lose their life for my sake, and for the sake of the gospel will save it."

Let's use this quote from the gospel of Mark (8:35) to talk about the role of the music minister in relationship to the parish community. Music can be a powerful tool in the liturgy for conversion, healing, teaching, and comfort, to name a few. But I want to emphasize the word "powerful." When hiring a musician, committees and clergy must know *what* they are looking for. If they hire someone to "give the people what they want," that is their choice. But if the only comment about the music is its beauty, then the music program is being shortchanged.

It is not a musician's task to simply "give them what they want." Music is formational. A musician works to fashion a people as much as any minister does. There will always be differences of taste, but a good program should include a wide variety of musical styles and forms regardless of the director's personal tastes. Committees and clergy need to realize this principle and allow the music director to stretch the assembly. We must stop fighting both the past and the future. Committees have every right to demand that texts speak to the present community. But a text is not irrelevant just because it is enfleshed in a past musical style. Nor are all texts or music from the past able to express the present and the future.

The issue is very complex. Is the musician to help fashion a people or to give people what they want? The choices are not mutually exclusive. They require one to "lose one's life," to give up some things for the sake of the gospel, and to find new life.

Hiring: How to Do It

In many parishes the ministry of pastoral music is growing from part-time positions into full-time employment. Consequently, more and more parishes — some for the first time — find themselves writing up job descriptions and conducting interviews with prospective directors of the ministry of music. Because this ministry affects the spiritual life of the entire parish, it is important to hire the right person.

Often a search committee is established. These committees have much to consider in their search for the right person. For example, a committee of college students in a university might choose a minister that they find really compatible, but the director and the staff have an equal need to be able to relate to and work with this person. The top priority for parish and musician alike is to achieve a mutually satisfactory arrangement.

With this in mind, it is crucial for the parish to define its needs clearly.

The Job Description. Job descriptions will vary from area to area and even from parish to parish. Some parishes want a musician/liturgist, while others want someone to handle music in worship and in the school. Other parishes might want to hire someone to introduce their communities to the world of music and the other arts, reminding them of the rich human cultural dimension that lies beyond our increasingly computerized and technological society. The job description must be as accurate as possible.

The interview and audition are just as important as the job description.

The Audition. There should be an audition. Schedule the musician for a rehearsal and not just a meeting with the other musicians. Demonstration is one of the best ways for a musician to win a position, and observation of the musician in action will prove very helpful.

The Interview. The interview is usually the final phase of the hiring process. This is when personalities, chemistry, and style all weigh heavily into the final decision.

It may be helpful for all parties (parish and musician) to consider several aspects of the interview that, when overlooked in the past, have resulted in disappointment for all concerned. For example, who will interview?

Who on the interviewing committee is qualified to ask the questions that need to be asked of a pastoral musician? The staff? The liturgy committee? Be sure the applicants are interviewed by a group of people who, for the most part, have some expertise in the area under discussion. Often the diocese can provide a resource person for you if you wish.

Shouldn't musicians take the major role in both audition and interview? Wouldn't it make sense to invite a successful pastoral musician from a nearby parish to help in the decision-making process?

I would also suggest that it is essential that you ask about your potential music minister's theology of celebration and how the musician would express that theology musically. Credentials look great on paper. Liturgical documents can be familiar to all concerned. But there is still one big gap in the discussion: STYLE. What musical style does the musician prefer? How does the musician express faith musically?

The Contract. How long a period does the contract cover? I've heard more than once of situations where the parish doesn't want to give a long contract, but then gets really upset when the musician leaves sooner than expected. Interview carefully!

On a practical level, will the musician have to relocate, moving and uprooting household and possibly children?

At its worst, the decision to hire will be based not on skill but on whether or not the musician will get along with everybody. It is so painful for both the musician and the parish when a wrong choice has been made. Better to find out sooner than later.

Last but not least, once you've hired someone, empower that person to do the job!

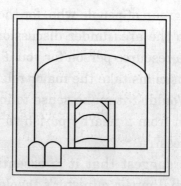

Cantors

Cantors, you are the ones who lead us in our affirmation of the living word as proclaimed by the lector. There's definitely more to being a cantor than getting in front and singing (reading?) to us. If the cantor is in front of the assembly but functions only as a voice delivering a text, then why bother? Go back to the loft! Cantors, you, too, must proclaim! Good proclamation commands the attention of the listener. If your presentation of the antiphon is not life-giving, then what can you expect from the assembly when they repeat the melody? Your proclamation must command attention in order to engage the assembly in their response. And the language you employ must be more than words; presence and gesture are essential.

First, about presence. Please don't get up and then pretend that you're invisible. And don't treat the assembly as if they're invisible. Communicate with them. You should know the music well enough to make eye contact with the assembly during all introductions and refrains. Pray the text when you sing it. Preach the text when you sing it. But for Pete's sake (or perhaps Paul's) don't just be a hollow gong or a clanging cymbal.

Second, use gesture. You need to do more than open your mouth wide (as if you were going to eat the microphone like an ice cream cone) in order to cue the assembly. Use your hands and arms — to breathe with and for the assembly. I sometimes observe cantors who simply lift an arm up into the air when it's time for the assembly to sing. Is this to find out which way the wind is blowing? The gesture must have purpose; it must clearly express when the assembly is to breathe so that they may come in together. Get a grip, folks. Know what you're about! Videotape yourselves once in a while.

Placement of Cantors

When cantors address us and sing from the choir loft, it can be unbelievably bizarre and sometimes very funny. But what liturgical confusion! Maybe you're not aware of this, but microphones, depending on their quality, often produce non-directional sound. If you spoke from the rear of the church without a microphone, we could discern where the sound was coming from. But sometimes when a person speaks through a microphone the sound comes from speakers placed around the room. And then we can't tell where the person is. If guests came to your church, and you were speaking to them from the choir loft above with a microphone that is non-directional, how would they discern where you were?

Cantors tell me that it's not always their choice to be in the loft. Someone has decided that it's distracting for the cantor to be seen. Based on that premise, perhaps we should put the presider and the lector up in the loft, too.

Now really, friends. Even God came to us enfleshed as a human being, not as a disembodied voice. Relying only on a microphone, you resemble something more like the Wizard of Oz than a cantor of our Judeo-Christian heritage. Help free Dorothy.

Feel free to mail this entry anonymously to whom it may concern.

Cantors: Performance or Ministry?

Someone pointed out to me that singing from the loft unseen is better than the "show" we witness in many churches when so-called cantors or song leaders "perform" down front. Here, here!

I don't think the solution lies in being unseen but in finding how ministry and performance differ. Good cantors don't just prepare music, they also devise a procedure to help the assembly learn their musical part. Cantors lead not only with voice but also with gestures for beginning, cues for ending, and guides for tempo. Leaders of song minister discreetly: there when needed, gone when not.

Cantors stand in front of the assembly for another reason. They communicate with the people they lead. Eye contact and facial expression give signals. Some music addresses God and some music addresses the people. Cantors sometimes reflect God's message to people in the style of the prophets, and sometimes they bear the prayers of the people to God in the style of intercessors. They must gesture to the assembly when it is time for the assembly to sing if they want the assembly to take their role as celebrators seriously. How rude it would be of cantors not to be gracious and inclusive of the primary celebrators of worship — the assembly.

The difference between performance and ministry is key. When members of the assembly say, "What a beautiful voice," they have heard a performance. But when they say, "We were moved by that psalm," they have been ministered to. Cantors and choirs enflesh the word of God the way readers enflesh it. Why do readers proclaim from the front?

We do not want performances in church. When cantors and choir members see themselves as animators of God's word rather than performers of music, they have less fear and sing more humbly and confidently. What if a reader, preacher, prophet, proclaimer, priest, or singer never looks at the people? Would that help? Why? Why not?

Cantors need to relate with members of the assembly as other ministers do. Can we muster courage to ask others for suggestions about our ministerial style?

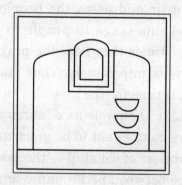

Guitarists

Some liturgical musicians (primarily the guitarists) in Raleigh, North Carolina, put together an examination of conscience for guitarists. They call it "The Guitar Confessional," but it's not for guitarists only! Some samples:

1) Can you hold a guitar without playing it? (Sound familiar?)

2) Do you invite participation?

3) Are you always flipping through music? Especially during the homily?

4) Do you practice intros and endings?

5) At Mass, can there be more than two songs without guitar without you pouting?

6) Can you play with other guitarists and musicians?

7) Do you pick keys that only Tiny Tim or the BeeGees can sing?

8) Can you relinquish control?

9) Do you plan your music for Mass in the car on the way there?

10) Do you see a title of a song in the readings and say "Eureka"?

11) Have you been doing the "Lilies of the Field" amen since 1969?

12) Do you play the same strings until they break?

Perhaps your group needs to atone for your offenses. Let the punishment fit the crime. But above all else, do not let the answers to these questions get into the wrong hands. You see, your assemblies probably think by now that some of these things are tradition. Or perhaps to know you is to love you. Other musicians, take note! Guitarists know that it's not good to take yourself too seriously.

Organists

This true story takes place in one of the warmer regions of our country where a friend of mine (who is a cantor) and her young family were vacationing. It's Sunday morning. The organ is up in front, piled high with books. The organist faces the assembly, but because of the pile of books all that my friend can see is the top of his head. This in itself would not be bad, except that then, from the bench, his voice addresses the assembly: "Good morning, everyone. I'm your new music director. Now, I don't know exactly what you've been singing up till now, but here's what we're going to sing from now on." And he then proceeds with his introduction and teaching.

What's wrong with this picture? My friend had the good sense to look toward the organ where she could at least see the top of the man's head bobbing as he spoke. But for the rest of the assembly it was a voice without a body. The only advantage to this would be that, if the congregation didn't like the new music or the director, they couldn't go after him because they wouldn't know what he looked like. But as liturgical ministry this isn't even close!

Preachers

I always thought that a homily was a post-Vatican II version of a sermon. Although in some ways it is, there's more to it than that. According to an entry by Father Robert Waznak, SS, in *The New Dictionary of Sacramental Worship*, a sermon is "not necessarily connected to the biblical readings and is heard outside the context of the liturgy." He observes, "Four characteristics of preaching were restored from the ancient tradition by Vatican II in order to distinguish this renewed form of preaching." Homiletic preaching is a) biblical, b) liturgical, c) kerygmatic, and d) familiar.

The first two characteristics are obvious: Preach on the readings during liturgy. The third characteristic, kerygmatic preaching, means proclamation. This is not preaching doctrine but proclaiming good news for the present time. Waznak, a professor of preaching, says that the Council "distinguished this form of preaching, which proclaims the wonderful things God has done and is doing for people, from preaching that is a list of dos and don'ts that we must follow in order to win God's favor."

The fourth characteristic is the reason it is called homily — a familiar conversation, a way of speaking from the heart. It is a conversation by a shepherd who knows the flock and is with them.

Not everyone is a gifted homilist. Preparation and reflection are key. Talent alone doesn't work. Preaching is one of the great privileges of the ordained. It should be taken very seriously. The homily forces the preacher to focus on a regular basis on the scripture of the week, on his life in relation to the scripture, on prayer, and on the needs of his community. The priest matures in his ministry and becomes more priestly through this kind of homiletic preparation. What is unfortunate about the priest who doesn't prepare (as Father Walter Burghardt, SJ, once said to me), is that none of this happens to him. Some wisdom, there.

Oh, by the way, preachers, we sometimes know when you're reading "canned homilies." At least put an attractive cover on them to keep us guessing.

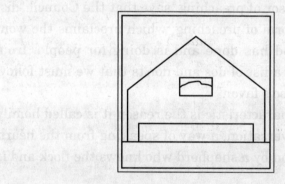

Eucharistic Ministers

It is important to understand the meaning of the word *special* when it is used in connection with liturgical ministries, eucharistic ministers in particular. The word *specialized* might be better than *special*. All liturgical ministers have a specialized task to do. Some read, some make music, some preach, some distribute communion, some take up the collection and manage the room. They are all specialized for one purpose or another. The words *special minister* were never meant to imply that one minister was more important than another — and certainly not more important than the assembly.

Sometimes it's difficult to recruit eucharistic ministers. This might be because of the name given the minister in the documents: *extraordinary minister of the eucharist*. This is not meant to describe in any way the personality or worthiness of the minister (although the description sometimes fits, for better or for worse, doesn't it?). According to *This Holy and Living Sacrifice: Directory for the Celebration and Reception of Communion under Both Kinds*, the *ordinary* ministers of the eucharist are bishop, priest, and deacon. "When there are large numbers of the faithful present . . . special or extraordinary ministers properly appointed beforehand should assist in the distribution of communion." Thus the prefix *extra-*.

Having the eucharistic ministers receive after the assembly is not meant in any way to diminish the role of the minister (if that should be a consideration). Rather, it is an attempt to show the gathered assembly that they are the primary celebrators, and that the rest of us ministers are servants. We will be last.

Readers

The entire assembly is called to active participation in the liturgy. "Participation" means "to take part." "Activity" is characterized by exertion of energy. Active participation, then, means that we must take part with an exertion of energy. Active participation demands that the lectors must do more than read to us from a book. If we are literate, we can do that for ourselves. Active participation on the part of the lector results in proclamation. And good proclamation commands the attention of the listener.

God's word is made flesh through the flesh of those present. God's spoken words become enfleshed for us through the lector. That's why we have lectors — not to help us read, but to be the "Word-bearers" for us. Language at liturgy communicates more than mere words. God is speaking through the lector, speaking to us today, right here and now.

Liturgy Preparation

Some liturgy planners are still preparing Mass by looking for themes and then selecting music that "fits the
theme." Yes, the readings contain messages and lessons for
us; they are a starting point for our liturgical preparation.
But readings are also symbols. And symbols can have a variety of meanings.

The story of the prodigal son (Luke 15:11–32) is an example of how scripture speaks to many people in many ways. On
the one hand there is the son who has caused his parents so
much pain. Then there are the parents, who grieved so over
the seemingly ungrateful and irresponsible son. Perhaps
"Where have I failed?" might be the cry that will resonate
with parents in our pews who find themselves in a similar situation. Or perhaps the estranged son himself is sitting in our
midst: "I was never close to my father. How do I know he'll
care if I call?" (Should we also tell the story of the prodigal
daughter? Preachers who have preached on the prodigal
daughter instead of the son say that the assembly gets very
engrossed. It's worth a thought.) And then, of course, there is
the "other" son . . . the righteous one: "I've been a good son all
these years, and look . . . they love that troublemaker more

than me . . . they always have." As much as we hate to admit it, we all can resonate a little with the touch of vengeance that this brother would like to see happen.

So what themes are you planning? Is everything focused on the prodigal son? The righteous people in the church who identify with the "other" son need attention and healing, too. Perhaps the little touch of vengeance hiding in our hearts needs to be expressed and put into the Lord's hands for transformation. Our psalms are excellent for this.

Here's the moral: The readings are rich and are meant to speak to many. Theme planning narrows the reading to a singular interpretation. Music and homilies should "break open" the readings, not narrow them.

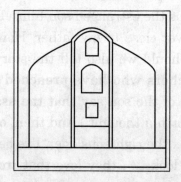

Not So Fast, Please

As liturgy/music ministry develops, and as ministers heighten and sharpen their musical skills and liturgical knowledge, the danger arises of wanting to implement change more quickly than the assembly can bear. Things will never move as quickly as musicians and liturgists wish they would. We don't live in a perfect world.

To force a parish to accept our ideas of liturgy and music makes us guilty of *the* mortal sin in ministry: serving our own needs rather than those of the assembly. The issue is not "to change or not to change," but how much change, how soon, and what methods we use to implement it.

Body Language

Pay attention to body language. Actions speak louder than words. The verbal language of liturgy is very beautiful, but it can be contradicted by body language. A stiff arm extended at the sign of peace, a musician who never looks at the assembly, people who sit with their arms crossed or with their faces in missalettes, ritualists who are more gentle with inanimate objects than with people — all these movements tell who we really are. On the other hand, warm handshakes, engaging cantors, gracious ministers of hospitality, and prayerful presiders all serve to enflesh the Word of the Lord and affirm the presence of Christ in our midst. Participation can only become fuller and richer if we concentrate on all the languages of liturgy.

Seek Radiance That Never Sleeps

If your liturgy group writes prayers, you might want to look for more lyrical and poetic approaches. Play with words that evoke images. Sometimes a powerful image can cut back tremendously on the wordiness of a prayer or intercession. Look at Wisdom 7:7–11, with its rich and vivid imagery, for inspiration.

And so I prayed, and understanding was given to me;
I entreated, and the spirit of Wisdom came to me.
I esteemed her more than scepters and thrones;
compared with her, I held riches as nothing.
I reckoned no priceless stone to be her peer,
for compared with her, all gold is a pinch of sand,
and beside her silver ranks as mud.
I loved her more than health or beauty,
preferred her to the light,
since her radiance never sleeps.
In her company all good things came to me,
at her hands riches not to be numbered.

(Jerusalem Bible)

Collaboration

"Team ministry" and "collaboration" are terms that we're hearing more and more frequently in our parishes. In her article on team ministry in *The New Dictionary of Sacramental Worship*, Dody Donnelly, SF, tells us that team ministry uses a circular rather than pyramid model of leadership in the service of the parish community. It is called a "circular" model because it focuses on human development rather than on power. "The goal of such a model," she says, "is the healing and reconciliation of persons and institutions working for change through a process of honest relationships, theological and pastoral training, and openness to being changed by that very process, therefore, conversion. It is a mirror of Jesus' own ministry with his apostles."

Six factors, says Sister Donnelly, are operative in team ministry:

1) *Consultation:* This means that people learn to ask for advice and help, both within and outside the team;

2) *Coalition:* Members of the team ally themselves with other groups with similar goals. This is especially true, says Donnelly, when ecumenical and inter-religious issues are involved;

3) *Organization:* Team members study, practice, and develop effective techniques for maintaining the organization and structure of the group;

4) *Referral:* Members of the team learn to be aware of the limits of their gifts and goals, in order to avoid over-extension and Messiah complexes;

5) *Representation:* "of the team, by and for the team, and of those they serve on the team";

6) *Participation:* Team members share decision making. They also share responsibility for roles and resources, and they share as well in both rewards and sufferings.

Who Should Choose the Music?

If you don't have problems between the liturgy people and the musicians in your parish, then spend this time giving thanks to God for the blessings you've received. If you do have troubles, then read on.

It is not the liturgy committee's responsibility to choose the music. Nor is it the professional liturgist's, *if* there is a competent pastoral musician available. There are exceptions, of course. But, generally speaking, we must allow musicians to do their job. Yes, we must collaborate, and yes, the musician must be open to input by members of the liturgy committee and the assembly. In the end, though, it is the musician who must accept responsibility for the success or failure of the music program.

I realize this topic can be a painful one for everyone involved. Musicians who work under these conditions are in great pain. If musicians don't choose the music in your parish, why is this so? Is it because they're incompetent? Is it because of differences of taste? The former is a legitimate reason. The latter is not. Could we at least begin to communicate some of the problems directly to one another in Christian truth and charity? Be up front about the problems. If it's not working, then it's not working. In all fairness, you should let the musicians do their job or else ask for their resignation. Be honest.

There are times when I, as a musician, must die to what I would like to see happen liturgically. But, if I am not the liturgy director, then I must be open and trust the expertise of the person in charge. Just because things aren't being done my way doesn't mean that they're wrong, or that the Spirit will not move through our liturgies. But letting go isn't easy.

We bring a lot of needless pain on ourselves by entering into a worship experience with expectations that things are supposed to happen in a certain way. All judgments should be put aside after the last rehearsal. During worship, we worship.

A Term of Office for Ministers?

Father John Shea, poet and storyteller par excellence (be sure to look up his writings in your favorite bookstore), tells a wonderful story about a woman who becomes a eucharistic minister. I asked him if he's published it and he said no. So I'll do my best to share some of what stuck with me when I heard him tell it. It deals with how this woman grows in her ministry over a period of about a year and a half. At first, she is focused on how she looks, and concerned with not dropping the host and such things. Months later, she remarks on the uniqueness of each person who comes to her communion station. Each one is so different. One even had tears in her eyes. After Mass the eucharistic minister approached the tearful woman, and they went for coffee and talked. In her time of ministry this eucharistic minister has grown to the point where she wants to reach out and physically touch the people who come to her for communion.

This story contains food for thought about the results of good ministry formation and the need for rotation of ministers. You might want to think about setting "terms of office" for those involved in ministry. Not because the current ministers are inadequate (though that may be the case), but because it gives others an opportunity to enter into a special journey of faith and love. As long as there are people who are "becoming" in the way that the lady in this story is "becoming," says Father Shea, then we are doing the right things in ministry.

If you are one of the ministers who should resign for a while, you must trust that the Lord will have an even better place for you. It can be a painful decision. Remember the words of John the Baptist from John 3:29–30: "The groom's best man waits there listening for him and is overjoyed to hear his voice. That is my joy, and it is complete. He must increase, while I must decrease."

Establish a firmly set length of service for ministers. The term need not be long but it should be a definite period. We should also be always looking for new faces to come into ministry for the very reasons that John Shea illustrates.

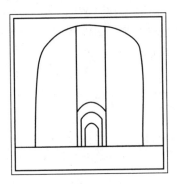

Part II

What We Do

4

The Eucharistic Liturgy

What Is Good Liturgy?

The first purpose of liturgy is to worship God and proclaim the good news. Unless we get down to these basics, we will continue the struggle between "conservative" and "liberal," "traditional" and "contemporary," *ad nauseam.*

Good liturgy enables conversion. No writer of church documents ever said that liturgy's goal is to help people go home "feeling good." "Feeling good" can result from an experience of conversion, but it is *conversion* that happens when the Holy Spirit moves in our midst. Life-giving celebration aids the work of the Spirit. Liturgy poorly celebrated can interfere.

Perhaps today someone will turn away from an addiction after the liturgical celebration. Certainly then the liturgy was a good one. It might be that for once the listener really heard God's word because it was proclaimed by an effective and prepared reader. Maybe the homilist, in speaking about the hungers of her or his own heart, broke open a common experience that allowed the Spirit to move someone.

Or maybe a person tried to heal a broken relationship by asking first, "How would Christ handle this?" or "What would Christ do here?"

Liturgy is formational. One of us might be moved to reconciliation by the words of the psalmist, who lamented the pain of sin and its resulting separation from God. Perhaps we dare dream about peace and justice in the world because our community encourages that response to the gospel message. Or maybe we were touched by one of God's people when we needed a hug, and were comforted enough finally to move on with our life. Ah, yes. Then we can truly say that it was a *very good liturgy*.

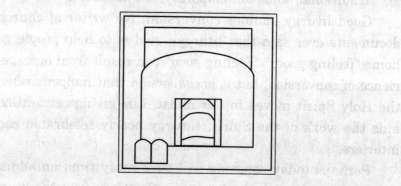

Mind and Heart at Worship

Like the covenant itself, the liturgical celebrations of the faith community (Church) involve the whole person. They are not purely religious or merely rational and intellectual exercises, but also human experiences calling on all human faculties: body, mind, senses, imagination, emotions, memory.

(Environment and Art in Catholic Worship, # 5)

In view of our culture's emphasis on reason, it is critically important for the Church to reemphasize a more total approach to the human person by opening up and developing the non-rational elements of liturgical celebration: the concerns for feelings of conversion, support, joy, repentance, trust, love, memory, movement, gesture, wonder.

(Environment and Art in Catholic Worship, # 35)

Most of our assemblies are to some extent "saying the words" and "singing the songs" on Sunday. This is great. Don't underestimate it. But there's more. Liturgy is not just a head trip. It should also involve the hearts and spirits of the people.

The purpose of language is to communicate. Many languages are used in liturgy, some verbal (the spoken word), some not (symbol, music, environment, and gesture, to name a few). I like to think of verbal communication as the language of the head, and non-verbal communication as the language of the heart. We ministers have all spent long hours preparing liturgies that nourish the cerebral dimension of ourselves — resulting in words, words, and more words at liturgy. But ministry involves integrating the mind and the heart.

Perhaps it's time to explore together the possibilities of involving the body, mind, senses, imagination, emotions, and memory. Begin by reading the document quoted above — in its entirety.

A Banquet Is Prepared . . .

One aspect of Sunday liturgy is that it is the heavenly banquet here in our midst — a foreshadowing of what is to come. Isaiah 25:6–10 prophesies about the feast that the Lord will provide on the mountain top for all peoples. The Lord Jesus, our host, has invited all of us to come together at Mass to share at his table. Our brothers and sisters in the community are there with us, those who have gone before us are with us, and Christ himself is present in the assembly, in the word, in the eucharist, in the priest. Some are called to welcome the guests at the table — as he would. Some are called to graciously serve the meal — as he would. Some will gently wipe away the tears from the faces of all those who suffer and grieve — as he would. Others are called to break down the divisions among people and gather them together at the table — as he did and does.

Psalm 23, one of the most popular of the psalms, is a beautiful psalm of comfort and consolation, and it is also about a banquet. The comfort and consolation aspect come from what will happen at the banquet. A table prepared . . . a banquet overflowing . . . family . . . friends.

Matthew 22:1–14 reminds us to live with a vision and keep our sights on the finish — a wedding banquet. Obviously, this will be no ordinary banquet. This parable of the heavenly banquet hints at the fullness of God's justice, mercy, and love.

Mass is not a memorial service. In liturgy, we remember into the future. Christ is redeeming the world NOW. We are stuck in time, but Christ is not.

Liturgy committees might explore the many times that Jesus dines in the scriptures. Talk about them with one another. Take time to talk with the assembly and the ministers about the importance of gathering, welcoming, and preparing ourselves as a community.

Honored Guests at the Table . . .

Let's look a bit more closely at Isaiah 25:6–10, which I mentioned in the previous reflection. It is a wonderful source of inspiration for those of us in ministry. If we image Sunday Mass as the banquet feast that Isaiah describes, perhaps our assemblies would understand better what we do at liturgy.

A paraphrase may help: In this house the Lord of hosts has provided a feast for us, the worthy and unworthy, the lame, the sick, the lonely, the brokenhearted, the sinners, the old, the young, the rich, the poor . . . a feast of rich food and choice wine prepared by servants here for all who are gathered . . . a house where each person is welcomed by all present just as the Lord receives us — as worthy, accepted, and loved. This is a house that serves the Lord . . . a house filled with people proclaiming and singing the praises of the Lord with all their minds and hearts. In this house we will work to destroy the veil that covers all of us — by offering hospitality to one another until the Lord comes to lift that veil completely from us and all nations. And we will wipe away the tears from the eyes of all who mourn in his name until the Lord comes again to wash away all tears completely and forever. We will forgive one another's faults as best as we are humanly able until the Lord God comes to show us wholeness and total forgiveness. And we will ask for forgiveness from our communal sinfulness, which only the Lord can grant. We will continue to say "Behold our God, to whom we looked to save us! The Lord for whom we look is here . . . in people, in word, in eucharist, in priest. Let us rejoice and be glad that God has sent Jesus to save us! Let us continue to gather here and remember . . . until we feast at the end of time on Zion, the holy mountain of the Lord in Jerusalem."

Deep apologies to Isaiah and theologians. I'm just trying to say it's here, it's now, it's real! Make the kingdom come! You are the voice of the living God!

Active Participation — Is Something Missing?

Active participation can be interpreted in several ways. The *Constitution on the Sacred Liturgy* invited the assembly to active participation in the spoken and sung responses of the liturgy. It also invited the laity to share in various liturgical ministries in ways unheard of in recent church history. We have made much progress in these areas. The singing is coming along, and in some places it's even great. The laity is becoming more and more involved in the liturgy. Yet, as I travel from town to town working with parishes, I notice that we talk a good game but we just don't "play" it that well. Let's look at one possible reason why.

If something life-giving is missing at liturgy, perhaps the celebration is a textual liturgy. A textual liturgy is one where everything is read to us. It begins with a "Good morning" that is read. Everything until "Please stand for the opening hymn" is read to us. And it sounds as boring as roll call in school. The opening prayer is read to us, as are the general intercessions and the eucharistic prayers. In many cases, the assembly reads along. And the musicians are reading their music — sight-reading in some cases.

Does any of this sound familiar? This is not celebration. This is not what our liturgy is meant to be.

Silence, Please

Active participation; incarnation; enfleshment of the word, music, and prayers in our ministry and in our daily life — all of these goals should be our constant companions. But there's one particular aspect of active participation that needs our special attention: silence and interiority. It's difficult for me to express this in liturgical language, so let me borrow from the world of music.

Just as rests (measured moments of silence) are essential to music, so there must be a balance between verbal and non-verbal communication in our liturgical celebrations. Musicians know that "rests" are poorly named. Rests punctuate the notes. Properly used, they help to convey meaning. Musical rests can express many things: humor, suspense, foreboding, surprise, awe, tension. Who could adequately describe in words a Grand Pause (⌒)? To proclaim is to communicate, and silence communicates.

We need to become more aware of the need for interiority and silence at Mass. In a metaphoric sense, does the use of silence speak as loudly as the spoken word in liturgy? Or do people "take a rest"? Does something active happen when we employ silence in our liturgies? Or are people merely relaxing?

Just as rests and notes work together to make music, verbal and non-verbal proclamation must work together to make liturgy. Ceremonial silence is one way to begin to help the assembly participate in the silence. Let symbols speak without explaining them. Processions with lights or banners (without words) that stay in place for a few moments are one way. Lighting incense and pausing before praying and moving with it are another.

Inclusive Language

The term "inclusive language" refers to words intentionally selected to redress the bias inherent in centuries-long use of language employed by the dominant culture. . . . It refers to the conscious substitutions of positive phrases in referring to people of color, instead of vilifying expressions like "blackmail." . . . It refers to words, therefore, which remove women from the invisibility and inferiority imposed upon them by such phrases as "mankind," "brotherhood of man." . . . And it refers to deliberately chosen words which refer to those who suffer patently observable impairments, calling them "mute" instead of "dumb," or "differently abled" instead of "disabled" or handicapped. . . . Inclusive language identifies the positive and equally important contributions of many different peoples and experiences. Inclusive language pertains to verbal and non-verbal images that describe both humankind and God.

— Janet Walton, "Inclusive Language,"
The New Dictionary of Sacramental Worship

Inclusive language attempts to do more than eliminate sexism in church and society. Let's look at the "feminine" language issues (Carl Jung might consider that a contradiction in terms since he considered language masculine), try to clarify some of the terms, and name some of the struggles.

There are currently two popular sexist language issues. Janet Walton refers to the first as the human or "horizontal" language. The second is theological or "vertical" language. In other words, the first deals with how we name people and the second deals with how we name God.

One of the most important aspects of inclusive language is that it be what it says: inclusive. To eliminate all references to the masculine is not inclusive. It is just as exclusive, offensive, and unjust as not including the feminine words. What we need is balance. Our Sacramentary tells the presider that he may make appropriate substitutions for the prescribed text where feasible in addressing his assembly (see footnote in *Sacramentary, Order of Mass, Penitential Rite*). For example, at the invitation before the Prayer Over the Gifts, he may say, "Pray, brothers and sisters" or "Pray, friends," instead of "Pray, brethren." Now some men might think this is a frivolous issue, but what if we reversed things and said, "Pray, sisters"? Wouldn't they feel excluded?

There are dioceses and parish communities that insist on "cleaning up" the sexist language. We must, in justice, begin. It doesn't take much effort to adjust texts so that "sons of God" becomes "sons and daughters of God" when proclaiming scripture. Liturgy committees should be wrestling with these issues. Have someone oversee this area.

Folks, some of this is easy. But most of it is difficult. And it really becomes complicated when we get into the area of how we name God. Ms. Walton states: "Male language limits the revelation of God." But so does the elimination of male language. We need both. We need to look for words that tell us that women, too, can be images of God. What saddens me is when amateurs play with the language, and mysteries such as the Trinity are reduced to the functionalism of "Glory be to the Creator, the Redeemer, and the Sanctifier." This may solve one problem but creates another. Let's hope we don't end up saying, "Glory Be to the Parent-Unit, the Offspring . . ."

Who Are You Talking To?

The problem of inclusive language can be a nightmare for poets and musicians. The pain of a male-dominated language system cannot always be corrected in lyrics as quickly as one might hope. There is also much pain inflicted on poets, lyricists, and melodists when the texts are adjusted by amateurs. For some, "Wash me and I shall be cleaner than snow" is an improvement; for others, it is painful. At a recent convention, "We are His people, the flock of the Lord" was changed to "We are God's people (so far, so good) the flock of our God." Ouch. This, at least, isn't as bad as changing to "We are your people." Why not? Because, in the original text we are singing to one another: "We are his people," or "We are God's people." When the pronoun "your" is substituted for "his," the psalm becomes directed to God and not to one another.

The Magnificat is the song Mary sang to her cousin Elizabeth about the wonders of God. Some versions of this canticle have been altered at the price of shifting the response from singing about God to singing to God. "My soul proclaims God's glory" is different from "My soul proclaims your glory."

I am not saying don't change words. I am simply asking for a heightened awareness of the complexity of the issues. We must recognize that language is just as much an art as music. I hope we have enough integrity not to alter the notes in a piece of music. We must have a similar sense of integrity when it comes to altering lyrics. This is not acceptable without the permission of the composer or the publisher.

5

Parts of the Mass

Gathering Rites

The first task of the assembly is to gather together. There is a big difference between gathering together and just being in the same room together. Gathering requires that we acknowledge the presence of one another as Christ among us. There may be new faces in your assembly weekly. Some people may have just moved into your area and are new to your parish. Others may be new to your particular liturgy. How can we include and welcome these folks so that no one is alone in our assemblies? Gathering is not a gimmick — it is crucial to liturgical celebration.

In the article "Gathering Rites" from *The New Dictionary of Sacramental Worship,* Kenneth Hannon, OMI, separates the function of gathering into three parts: 1) welcome/arrival, 2) establishment of identity, and 3) beginning/opening. He feels that the welcoming part of our liturgy — the welcoming of members, visitors, and strangers — belongs at the point of arrival. This wouldn't be essential in a town where everyone knew everyone, but it is necessary in most of today's parish communities. If it is true that there are parishes where members don't see one another from week to week except at liturgy, then the welcome and greeting become even more important. Father Hannon states, "Liturgically apt hospitality goes beyond the merely warm reception and seeks to express reverence for the person and for the event." It is not the same as the kiss of peace, nor is it a "howdy, neighbor" time.

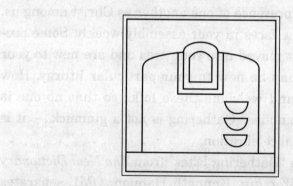

Some "Welcome" Help

Here are a few sample "lead-ins" to help with the welcome, so people will understand its liturgical purpose. Memorize them. Try to avoid reading them.

Ordinary Time

· Jesus tells us to welcome the stranger. So that there are no strangers in our midst, please turn and welcome the people around you.

· Jesus said, "He who welcomes me welcomes the One who sent me." Let us greet Christ in one another by welcoming those around us.

· We come together from many places in our life journey. Some here are living with joy and new life, and others are experiencing pain. But, so that no one is alone on the journey, please turn and welcome the people around you.

· We come together today as sons and daughters of the Lord at his table. Let us welcome one another as honored guests in God's house.

· We come together here today to celebrate a foretaste of the heavenly banquet where someday everyone will be greeted by Christ as our host. Let us be Christ for one another by welcoming one another to this holy house.

· As a sign of our unity in Christ Jesus, that we might pray, sing, and celebrate as one, let us introduce ourselves to the people around us.

· We come together from many places in our journey of life. That we may be one together in our joy and sorrow, please greet one another as the family of God.

Of course, lead-ins can be more specifically geared to the seasons of the liturgical year. Feel free to adapt them to your own needs. Some appropriate seasonal greetings might take the following form:

Advent

· As winter nights grow longer and days shorter, in our Advent liturgies we proclaim light against darkness, warmth against cold, and hope against despair. Let us welcome our neighbors as we would welcome Christ.

· We are God's people, called to be light and hope for one another. As brothers and sisters who wait together for the light that darkness cannot overcome, let us turn to greet one another.

Christmas

· Good evening (morning), and welcome to our parish eucharistic celebration. We have traveled from many places to be here together on this great feast of the birth of our Lord. Some have come home from college. Some have journeyed far and long in their life to this hour. Some are with loved ones — and some are without them for the first time. But here and now there may be no strangers. As brothers and sisters of Jesus our newborn Savior, let us turn to welcome one another.

Lent

· *(especially First Sunday)* During Lent we are called to prayer. We must go to our secret places to pray alone, and we also pray together. In preparation for our common prayer, let us welcome one another.

· *(especially Second Sunday)* Today we celebrate the Lord transfigured. As companions on the way with Christ to the mountaintop, let us be in union with one another. Please greet your neighbor.

· *(early Lent)* We are called to be a reconciled and reconciling people. We begin our journey by reaching out to those around us. Please welcome one another as brothers and sisters in Christ.

· *(later Lent)* At the Easter Vigil new members will enter our Christian community. Let us celebrate our own and their approaching full participation at the Lord's table by extending a welcome to those around us.

Easter

· Christ is risen. Alleluia! On this magnificent feast, please welcome those around you, especially the visitors.

(Special occasions lend themselves to special welcomes. Elsewhere in this book see "Some 'Welcome' Help for Masses with Baptisms," page 135, and "Active Participation at Weddings," page 153, for some suggestions.)

The welcoming can be done by the musician (or any other appropriate minister). Take a few moments before the first song to do this. Note how the singing and participation improve after the assembly members greet one another.

Gathering Song

We've all heard the jokes about entrance songs. You know, ones like "Please stand and greet our celebrant in song with 'O Come, O Come Emmanuel' (or 'Come Down, O Love Divine')." And then, of course, there's a lot of consternation from presiders who want musicians to stop introducing the opening song with "Please stand and greet our celebrant in song with 'Come, Holy Ghost' (or worse yet, 'Hail, Holy Queen')." Why don't people laugh outright when we say things like this? I wonder if they hear any of what we say. Or if *we* do.

Well, I heard a new one. The opening song in one cathedral church for the First Sunday of Lent was "Silence! Frenzied, Unclean Spirit." Now, really! This song fit perfectly with the theme of the day, but doesn't it seem rather inappropriate that the very first words out of the mouths of the assembly on a Sunday would be addressed to the evil one? I think we've got to be more attentive to the text of the opening song. We are there first and foremost to praise God — not to establish themes.

Processions

It's time that we take a serious look at the use of the procession in our liturgies, particularly the entrance procession. A procession is a ceremonial movement of a group of people from one place to another for some specific purpose. Processions have occurred in our church history as a means of Christian witness, as acts of penitence or praise, or as acts of supplication. Some are integral parts of the rites — the procession of the gifts at eucharist, to the font at baptism, or to the grave at burial, for example. Each of these has a practical purpose. But what is the purpose of the entrance procession?

It seems to me that when the cross of Christ Jesus — the most powerful sign of who we are — is carried through our midst, we become the people of God at prayer. The entrance procession serves this function. Composer Lucien Deiss suggests that when the priest joins the community in the entrance procession, it then becomes the liturgical community because, as the *Constitution on the Sacred Liturgy* (#33) says, the priest presides over the assembly in the person of Christ.

At any rate, the entrance procession is meant to be functional as well as festive. One cross-bearer, one book-bearer, and one presider are the essentials. After all, the worshipers in the pews are the primary celebrators of the liturgy. Any special minister, whether it be reader, eucharistic minister, usher, or musician, should come forth from those pews and be identified as a member of the assembly. There is no need to include them in the procession. To do so separates the people of God into "doers" and "receivers," "management" and "clients," "performers" and "audience."

Processions that have purpose and function are fine. Processions that emphasize certain people or roles have no place in liturgy. Down with egos! Up with full participation of the assembly!

Signs of Reverence/Bows

New ministers usually have questions about making signs of reverence to the altar or tabernacle when they take part in the entrance procession. For the record, the *Ceremonial of Bishops* (#70) tells us that "neither a genuflection nor a deep bow is made by those who are carrying articles used in a celebration, for example, the cross, candlesticks, the Book of the Gospels." Article 71 says that those who pass before the blessed sacrament genuflect except when they are walking in procession.

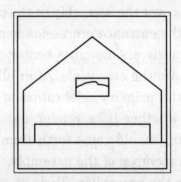

Greeting

Many of you are probably familiar with the conversations surrounding the book *Why Catholics Can't Sing* by Thomas Day. I took part in a debate about it at an annual convention of the National Association of Pastoral Musicians. The book irritated me because it drew outrageous (in my humble opinion) conclusions to some valid issues. But some of those valid issues need our attention.

In one section of the book Day complains about the informality of our liturgies. He describes the lofty, triumphant opening hymn, followed by the mundane "Good morning." Sound familiar? Although not every liturgy begins this way, most entrance rites are similarly fashioned.

Attention, presiders: We know that over the years many of you have worked hard to enflesh the liturgy into a prayerful liturgy not only of transcendence but also of truly human celebration. But let's take another look. The new liturgy is supposed to eliminate the verbosity, redundancy, and repetition of the old one. Aren't you saying two greetings when you say "Good morning," following "The grace and peace of the Lord Jesus Christ be with you"? Isn't the latter, which uses ritual language, much more significant and encompassing than the former, which is limited and mundane? What better greeting could there be than one of the ritual greetings from the Roman Missal or the *Book of Blessings*?

Think about memorizing these greetings. Say them with energy. Speak your greeting from your heart. Make the greeting come alive. Isn't that why we slipped into "Good morning" in the first place?

Penitential Rite

Many people interpret the penitential rite to be an examination of conscience. It is not. The *General Instruction of the Roman Missal* (#29) tells us that the penitential rite is made up of a communal confession, which the priest's absolution brings to an end. We acknowledge that we are sinners. Not *moi, nous*. All of us. We the community. Not just me.

Our assemblies need to understand the communal aspect of this rite and develop a clearer understanding of its introductory nature. After a greeting and opening song, which attempt to "collect" a roomful of individuals into a united, praying assembly, why would our introductory rites invite people back into introspection through an examination of conscience? The rites don't. Pastoral practice does, and this is in need of some rethinking.

Liturgy committees: Take a look at all the forms of the penitential rite and read them carefully. Use all the options, but know what you are doing — and why. For example, one form of the penitential rite contains the *Confiteor* ("I confess to almighty God . . . "). This is a remnant from the prayers at the foot of the altar of the Latin Mass. Not only is it individualistic, it is lengthy. It becomes even more disproportionate within a rite considered *introductory* if it is preceded by a "mini-examination of conscience" that also includes a period of silence. This may be why many liturgists feel that it is a weak form.

Glory to God / Gloria

The *General Instruction of the Roman Missal* (#31) tells us that the Gloria may be sung by the congregation, or by the congregation alternately with the choir, or by the choir alone.

You might want to sing the Gloria as the processional during Christmas. If so, please use a musical setting that includes the people; the gathering song should be an assembly song. If, however, you choose to sing it just before the opening prayer, then musical settings from the classical repertoire in English or in Latin may be used as long as the one chosen is not too lengthy. Latin may be surprisingly helpful, especially if your parish is bilingual or multilingual.

During Christmastime, parishes with limited musical resources might consider using the "Gloria in excelsis Deo" refrain from the French carol, "Angels We Have Heard On High" as a repeated refrain interspersed throughout a recitation of the Gloria. For example:

Sing the refrain: "Gloria in excelsis Deo . . . "

Then recite: "Glory to God in the highest . . . we praise you for your glory."

Then sing: "Gloria in excelsis Deo . . . "

Then recite: "Lord, Jesus Christ, only Son . . . receive our prayer."

Then sing: "Gloria in excelsis Deo . . . "

Then recite: "For you alone are the Holy One . . . in the glory of God the Father. Amen."

Then sing: "Gloria in excelsis Deo . . . "

It can be sung without accompaniment. If you are using accompaniment, use no introduction during the interior antiphons. If you can rehearse some basic chord progression to play softly between verses, go for it. It'll make the transitions much smoother. (This suggestion is not meant for use as a processional, but after the penitential rite.)

Opening Prayer

Last but not least — the opening prayer. Remember: "Let us pray" should be a call for silent prayer. It should not be a cue for the acolyte to go get the Sacramentary.

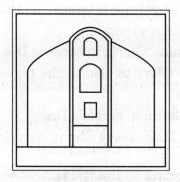

Checklist for the Opening Rites

The Liturgy of the Word begins with the first reading. In some parishes, because the introductory rites are so exaggerated, the first reading is where the assembly sits down to take a rest. What do I mean by exaggerated? If you can answer "yes" to any one of the following questions, your liturgy group needs to tailor the introductory rites:

1. Do you greet and gather the assembly more than once (e.g., the musicians gather, the lector welcomes, then we sing the gathering song, after which the presider says "Good morning," and then greets everyone again)?

2. Do you announce the names of all the ministers (lectors, gift bearers, etc.)? If so, besides taking time for introductions, what does this say about the assembly as the chief celebrators?

3. Do you sing all the options for the introductory rites (e.g., gathering song, Lord, have mercy [Kyrie], Glory to God [Gloria])? If so, do these musical moments overshadow the readings and the psalm?

Readings

How might readers of the word prepare for their ministry? How might they break open the readings either for themselves or in a group? Here's a suggestion, using the readings for the Second Sunday of Advent, Cycle C (Lectionary #6) as an example.

In the first reading from Baruch (5:1–9) think about how "Jerusalem" stands for God's people — and we are those people. Lectors, read that Hebrew Testament passage to your assembly not as a piece of historical information, but as good news for their lives. When practicing the text, substitute the phrase "People of (parish name) community" instead of "Jerusalem." The second reading (Philippians 1:4–6;8–11) is a letter and may be read more like a letter. Presiders might substitute the parish's name for "disciples" when practicing the gospel (Luke 3:1–6).

Be careful, though. Not all readings will work like this. And not all readings bear the same weight. But, especially in Advent, proclaimers of the word might reflect on what it means to be "Word-bearers."

Psalms

The responsorial psalm should be the musical centerpiece of the Liturgy of the Word. When will musicians stop teaching musical "ditties" for responsorials? These kinds of antiphons will be gone from people's heads and hearts even before they hit the parking lot to go home. The responsorial psalm is the assembly's acclamation of the proclamation of God's Word in our midst. That is how we worship: proclamation followed by acclamation.

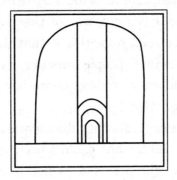

Praying the Psalms

Psalms are one of our oldest forms of prayer. They are the way that Jesus prayed. Psalms express the range of human emotions. Maybe the reason we don't entirely appreciate them is that we don't really know how to use them. When we pray a psalm, we express many of the same sentiments that centuries of people who have gone before us have also expressed. There is great comfort in knowing that so many before us have had these same longings, fears, hopes, and joys. It can strengthen our faith.

For some solid insight written for lay persons like us, get hold of Walter Brueggemann's *Praying the Psalms*. I would like to share a few of his points with you for our own learning and to encourage you to use his book as a text for your cantors, liturgy committees, music groups, and homilists.

Brueggemann suggests that we move with God in our life journey in three ways: 1) being securely oriented; 2) being painfully disoriented; and 3) being surprisingly reoriented. He contends that the driving power of the psalms comes from points 2 and 3. The reason for this is that the psalms are passionate expressions from people who are crying out "from the edge." In his words, they are "eloquence born of passion which is turned to the Holy One."

Brueggemann suggests that disorientation (his point 2) is best expressed in the lament psalms (cf. Psalm 22). They are the voice "of those who are mad as hell and are not going to take it anymore." The psalmist in this type of psalm talks about being forgotten, silent, dead, depressed, cut off, etc. Any reference to being "in the pit" contains these feelings (see Psalms 13, 88). And not only do we want to be saved from the "pit," but we want others to be sent there . . . a seemingly strange thought for a good Catholic!

Then, at some point in our lives, we may find ourselves

surprisingly reoriented with God (Brueggemann's point 3). The surprise reorientation is a great change from the status quo. It might be finding a new friend in our life, or a reconciliation in a lost relationship. In these situations we connect with Israel's psalms of thanksgiving and praise.

A prominent image of this reorientation in the psalms of thanksgiving and praise is that of being "under safe wings." Those wings convey safety, tenderness, refuge, nurturing, and well-being. Images such as the fortress, the tower, the rock, and the shelter also help trigger our imaginations in this direction. Psalm 17, David's song of victory, is a good example of this type of psalm.

Some of these psalms of thanksgiving and praise are not necessarily hymns of reality, but are evocative of a reality. Brueggemann calls the celebrative psalms "acts of radical hope." So, in Psalm 8, for example, we sing, "How great is your name O Lord our God, through all the earth." But that text is not a reality. Not everyone praises God's name. But it is evocative of a reality. We believe in a future where everyone will sing "how great is your name . . . ."

Want to try an exercise for praying the psalms? Imagine that someone has hurt you badly and you are very angry (not unlike the psalmist in Psalm 109, verse 1–20). Now read Psalm 109 from verse 21 to the end. It's OK to be angry in front of God. The good news is that when you voice your angry words and hand them to God, God will transform your anger.

Obviously, not all of us are "at the edge" on Sunday mornings. But some folks are. If the responsorial psalm for that day is a lament, those who are "in the pit" or "filled with tears" will relate well to the psalm. If the psalm is a psalm of praise, those who are experiencing new life will sing out. But even those who are not "at the edge" still need to be prepared for the edge. As Brueggemann says, "our lives always move from 'pit' to 'wing.'"

Psalms and Assemblies: A Few Observations

1) Assemblies would do well to learn several lament and thanksgiving psalms by heart so that they might pray them when they need them. People need psalms at home and work as well as in church.

2) Teach psalms that have a strong melody. This will enflesh the texts and help people remember the words.

3) Begin a five-year plan for teaching psalms. Then proceed to teach eight to ten psalms a year. That's a lot of psalms in five years. Start with the psalms the assembly will need for the liturgies of the more solemn seasons — Advent/Christmas, Lent/Easter.

4) There is still a great need for composers to create psalm settings that express the passion of the psalms. The texts of the psalms can spark our imagination in so many ways. Shouldn't the musical notes reinforce that imagination?

5) Teach psalms to our children. If children can learn foreign languages, poetry, and math by the age of four, then why do we continue to underestimate their ability to sing psalms? They will remember the psalms they learned as children for the rest of their lives. Psalms will see children through a lifetime of emotions and experiences. And psalms will teach them to pray in connection with a long line of ancestors (Jesus included).

6) Go out and buy Brueggemann's book *Praying the Psalms*. If you already own it, read it again. Outline it and use it as the basis for instruction of your assembly. When you teach a psalm on Sunday, it will be better received if the assembly has some understanding of how a psalm should work. For example, if I am working with children (of any age), I might say, "Today we will learn Psalm 23, which talks of a banquet that is prepared for each of us. As we sing, try to think of all the times that you've sat at a table and experienced wonderful food and conversation or reconciliation or love."

7) Psalm 23, "The Lord is My Shepherd" is not the only psalm in the psalter. There are 150 psalms. Our assemblies don't need five versions of this one. How about Psalm 22? Or 24? They're pretty good, too.

On Good Shepherd Sunday it's not a good idea to sing all possible versions of the Twenty-third Psalm. Yes, they're all beautiful and the people should hear them. So why not sing a different version on Sundays during communion? The psalm is about a banquet and is always appropriate at Eucharist.

8) From what part of the church should the responsorial psalm be sung? Take up this question with the experts. There are just as many opinions as experts. My response? Go where you can best be in communication with the people of God . . . and the accompanist.

General Intercessions

One area that sometimes can be a problem is the response to the general intercessions. Some of the creative, thematic responses can be pretty funny. What keeps the people from laughing out loud? David Haas tells the story of the church that responded, "Spare Us, O Lord" to the petitions. This worked fine until about the fifth petition, when someone prayed for world peace. Hmm!

Please. Pay attention to what is going on.

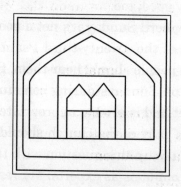

Acclamations

Music in Catholic Worship (MCW) tells us (#53) that acclamations are "shouts of joy which arise from the whole assembly as forceful and meaningful assents to God's Word and Action." The acclamations are: the Alleluia before the Gospel, the Holy, the Memorial Acclamation, the Great Amen, and the Doxology to the Lord's Prayer. MCW further states (#54) that "acclamations ought to be sung even at Masses in which little else is sung."

Gospel Acclamation

Acclamations should not have introductions, especially when they affirm or continue what goes before (such as in the Holy following the preface). These acclamations should not *need* introductions. The gospel acclamation is a little different. It is both a "reflection upon the Word of God proclaimed in the liturgy and a preparation for the Gospel" (MCW #55). Whereas the focus of the psalm is the text, the essence of the gospel acclamation is the *music*. It should express the joy that is contained in the word *Alleluia*. Musical problems can arise when the musician is confronted with introductions to acclamations, but these problems lend themselves to creative solutions.

Sanctus/Holy, Holy

Use the same Holy seasonally — simply give a starting pitch or chord to the assembly. Yes, I said change the Holy *seasonally*. And I mean seasonally *at most*. Keep in mind that the *Lutheran Book of Worship* uses only a few

"Ordinaries" in the entire book. That's all. People don't need a different Holy each week. If the music is well constructed, the assembly will not tire of it. Furthermore, they should not have to look up the music in a book in order to respond. It is best to know it by heart. The *worst* offense, however, is to announce the page number just before they sing. Do you know what I'm talking about? Just as Father finishes saying, "And so we join with the angels and archangels in their unending hymn of praise . . . ," someone says: "Page 96, number 2 . . ." and so it goes. Sound familiar? I hope not.

Another solution to the problem of intros is to start the music to the Holy softly (not to be confused with slowly) while the priest is inviting us to join with him and the angels in one unending hymn of praise. This solution involves musical sensitivity and discretion. When music is introduced at this point, we need the priest to speak a little louder so that the words and the music combine graciously to heighten the intensity of the text and extend the invitation to the assembly to sing meaningfully and full-heartedly when it is time for their entrance. If the priest and the musician are not relating lyrically to each other, the music can seem to be an intrusion on the recitation of the priest's part of the preface. The issue here is not a question of the use of music, but one of lyrical relationship and balance within a musical/liturgical moment.

The same techniques of musical liturgy are also encouraged for the memorial acclamation and the Amen to the doxology.

Breaking of the Bread / Lamb of God

It is clear to me that our people need eucharistic catechesis. Many of you have asked me at workshops how you might help your assembly to understand the eucharist and the eucharistic prayer. Here are some of my thoughts.

The best way to handle this is through preaching. Part of the homily might be spent on catechesis of the communion rite.

It is in the breaking of the bread that the disciples recognized Jesus. It is a holy moment in our liturgy, a moment of awe and silence. It is our moment of unity. Obviously, we should all be doing the same thing. Not ushering, not looking for music, not figuring out communion stations, but being in wonder that the Lamb of God should love us so much that he lays down his life for us and takes away the sin of the world. And we respond, "Lord, I am not worthy . . . ."

Someone once told me that she didn't like to pray that response because she had spent her whole life thinking she was unworthy and was only just beginning to feel "OK" about herself after three years in therapy. Folks, this prayer has nothing to do with personal worthiness. It has to do with the fact that because of Christ, we, too, become part of the divine. And certainly that's nothing we ourselves can do, nor are we worthy to become. It is pure gift and grace. In some churches there's so much commotion at this time of communion preparation that if Jesus walked down the aisle, someone would probably direct him to a communion line, give him a songsheet, and most of the other members of the assembly wouldn't even notice. In other churches, people are so wrapped up in their personal preparation for communion, they wouldn't notice him either. (Did you ever wonder if Jesus was a tenor or a bass?) What about at your liturgies?

Communion Processionals

I have frequently been asked how I handle the issue of when and how musicians might receive communion. This can be a real problem because the singing of the communion processional/song is essential to good liturgical practice. Why? Because singing together is a sign of the unity of the assembly as they come to receive the sacrament of unity. It is a symbol of our unity with God but also with one another. According to the *General Instruction* (#56i), the communion song should be sung "during the priest's and the faithful's reception of communion . . . . Its function is to express outwardly the communicants' union in spirit by means of the unity of their voices, to give evidence of joy of heart, and to make the procession to receive Christ's body more fully an act of community." We must pay attention to the horizontal as well as the vertical dimension of communion.

If the communion song is simple, with an easy antiphon or refrain, the choir will have less difficulty processing to communion. It is important to instruct them to keep singing as they process. Have a soloist or cantor prepared to do some of the verses of the communion processional alone if necessary. But usually there's no need for the choir to stop singing. Singers tend to have refrains memorized anyway. Perhaps memorizing the refrains with their harmonies and descants might become a regular part of your rehearsal procedures. However, if you are still singing hymns with lots of changing texts, you can expect to have problems. How on earth can we expect the assembly to sing while in procession to the table if our choirs can't do it?

If your music group prepares anthems or motets to sing during communion, this music must take a secondary place to the communion processional of the assembly. Sing an assembly communion psalm or song first, then follow it with a bit of instrumental music, and then lead into the choir anthem. You need not wait until communion is finished to begin the anthem. Just because some people are still walking around doesn't mean they aren't listening.

Communion Procedures for Musicians

Here are some more suggestions on procedures for musicians to receive communion. Depending on the size of the choir, the size of the assembly, and the occasion, getting everybody to communion is not an easy task. I also worry about people tripping over equipment and cords. Here's how I initiated a system that eventually became the norm at my church.

Once, when there was a very special occasion involving large numbers of people, I requested ministers of the eucharist whose sole responsibility was to take care of distributing bread and cup to the musicians. We asked spouses of musicians to do this since they are special to us and understand our difficulties. (I realize that sometimes diocesan legislation won't allow this.) These ministers simply "stood by" until I gave the signal to begin distribution. Distribution began toward the end of the first communion processional, which began, of course, immediately after the presider received eucharist.

(This "stand by" approach came about as a result of one unfortunate occasion when I was involved playing an intricate keyboard accompaniment and was busy watching my music. I didn't look up, but my ears told me something not good was happening. When I finally did look up, I noticed that the entire soprano section was dropping out of the song, one by one, as they received communion. And the ministers were now heading toward the alto section. What a disaster! So our solution goes like this: song, instrumental music while choir receives, and then second song.)

Musical Texts for Communion

I mentioned before that some psalms are perfect communion hymns. What about other types of hymns? I am often asked if Marian hymns can be used at communion. Fortunately, I have the opinion of the Bishops' Committee on the Liturgy on this question. To wit:

Music used for communion should be either a psalm or an appropriate hymn. This hymn should be Christological in character even when it reflects the season of the Church year. Marian hymns are appropriate only when they focus on Christ or at least relate to Mary as the Mother of God and not merely praise Mary in isolation from her role as *Theotokos* (Christ-bearer). A Marian hymn might be appropriate at the entrance or during the preparation of the gifts, but not during the distribution of communion.

The text of the Magnificat, with its appropriate antiphon, is a way of integrating Mary's words with a focus on the Lord. We are encouraged to take a renewed look at Mary as a symbol of justice and identify her with the struggles of the poor and oppressed.

Dismissal

Ite missa est (translation: "Go, the Mass is ended"). The Roman rite gives three choices for dismissal: A) Go in the peace of Christ; B) The Mass is ended, go in peace; C) Go in peace to love and serve the Lord. Not one says "and have a nice day." What we do at this point in liturgy is very serious. We are sent forth — missioned. The dismissal is a beginning, not an ending. The people in the pews are sent out as disciples into the marketplace, the office, the classroom, the hospital, skid row, the halfway houses, the homeless shelters — to anywhere where the good news must be proclaimed and Christ made present. That is the mission of the assembly. Cutesy endings such as "Have a nice day" diminish the power of the rite. Again, the answer is not to add more words to the rite, but for the presider to actively participate in the rite by saying these words with meaning.

This may seem like a small point. But by putting all of these small points together, we end up with one very "clubby" liturgy that begins and ends with us making ourselves "feel good." Cutesiness belongs somewhere, but not in liturgy! Send us forth as if you are Christ speaking to his disciples. Urge. Plead. Command. Lead. Challenge.

6

Masses with Children

Where To Begin

There are two essential sources for those working with the preparation and celebration of the eucharist with children. The first is the *General Instruction of the Roman Missal* (GIRM). The second is the *Directory for Masses with Children* (DMC). The DMC is geared toward children who have reached the age of catechesis and is intended to be used as a supplement to the *General Instruction*. It is divided into an introduction and three main chapters: Chapter I is the introduction of children to the eucharistic celebration; Chapter II deals with Masses with adults in which children also participate; and Chapter III covers Masses with children in which only a few adults participate. I call this "Masses with mostly children."

Here is an important distinction — while both types of experiences are valuable for children, the DMC suggests that Masses with children in which only a few adults participate *take place during the week.*

Masses with Children:
Where Do We Go From Here?

I would like to challenge two currently popular models for Masses with children. The first is the entertainment model; the second is the catechetical model. Neither one really helps children become primary celebrators of the eucharist.

In the entertainment model, children (and in most cases parents, too) come to liturgy to be entertained. This is not to say that we shouldn't work to break open the Liturgy of the Word for children through drama, visuals, and other methods. But this model propagates the false notion that liturgy is something that is done for us and to us. It reinforces a model of liturgy that we're trying to discourage — that of the ministers as the "doers" and the assembly as the "receivers."

The catechetical model attempts to extract a single message from the liturgy of the day, and then drives this message home from the time the Mass begins till it ends. It's a "left-brain" approach to liturgy — verbal and rational. The implementation of this style takes the form of music, prayers, and actions that reinforce the chosen theme. Liturgy is formational, but formation is different from catechesis.

According to *Environment and Art in Catholic Worship* (EACW), "Each church gathers regularly to praise and thank God, to remember and make present God's great deeds, to offer common prayer, to realize and celebrate the kingdom of peace and justice."

A clear and simple way of presenting that definition to children is this: The reason we go to Mass is to praise God and to experience God's love for us in Jesus Christ.

"Why Do I Have to Go to Church?"

How can we tell children about what's going on at Mass? Try this.

When Christ was on the earth in human form he loved people. He cried with them in their times of sorrow, he went fishing, boating, and hung out at the beach with them. He played with their children, forgave them when they were unkind to him, and even got angry with them when they weren't doing their best at being human. Jesus celebrated life with them.

We do this by gathering together and welcoming one another as brothers and sisters in the Lord. After that we sit down and listen to the stories of how God saves the people and how Jesus lived and how we should live. Then we give thanks and remember that Jesus gave his life for us. We remember all those who are living who need God, and we ask the saints and angels and all our beloved dead to be present with us. After the Lord's prayer we receive the body and blood of our Lord and Savior. Finally, we are sent forth to love and serve the Lord.

Liturgy and Religious Education

A few words about liturgy and religious education. The organization of a parish is a very individualized, sometimes compartmentalized, intricate combination of committees, subcommittees, and who knows what else. The liturgy/worship committee somehow manages to reach out to many of these groups. In my experience, however, one group that seems to fall in the cracks is the department for religious education of the children. It is becoming clearer and clearer to me that the liturgist/musician must become involved with the religious education program. And it is most important that the teachers of these groups have some instruction in liturgy. The religious education of our children has come a long way since the reforms of Vatican II. However, those children who were caught in the confusion of the old and the new happen to be the parents of the children we are teaching right now. Twenty years ago the liturgical/musical education of the parents was very limited. The new music was just beginning to develop. (I shudder to think how shallow was the well of post-Vatican II liturgical music back then.) But let's face it. How can we get children to understand what liturgy is about if the parents and the teachers aren't kept informed? Getting the adults involved in their children's religious education is our primary challenge.

I realize that many parishes have solved this problem. But I still strongly recommend that the religious educators have a session on liturgy at least once a year. Don't tell me there isn't enough time. The textbook curriculum must make room for the liturgy. Liturgy forms us. Unfortunately, liturgical celebrations sometimes end up looking more like textbook lessons than celebrations. Perhaps the music person could talk to parents about the importance of liturgical/musical formation and the reasons for it. It is up to your liturgy committees to take a look at this problem.

What Are We Teaching the Children?

Some parishes have a Sunday liturgy that is "performed" by the children, that is, the children are the readers, the intercessors, the choir. The children make announcements and take up the collection. (It's interesting that they don't handle the eucharist.) Is it possible that we are teaching these children that liturgy is only for kids and that when they grow up they might become passive spectators like their parents before them? And so we return to the original and basic challenge: *getting the adults involved.*

Liturgies with children can be very rewarding. But in the long run, parents sharing and witnessing their faith with their children will be even more rewarding.

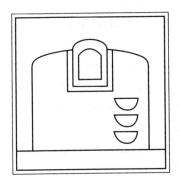

Parents Are the Primary Teachers

Adults must be made aware of the very active and important role they play in their children's formation at liturgy. Children learn values from their parents. Adults need to help the children sing, include them in the welcome and gathering rite, help them to be still and pay attention at sacred moments (even when they don't understand what's going on), touch them, teach them how to use silence, and show them how to pray meaningfully and with energy (even if they don't "feel" like it).

For those of you who might think I need a reality check at this point, fear not. I know everybody's situation is different, but let's get down to two basic questions: What is it that we're trying to do with children at liturgy? Are we going at it with the proper vision?

Although liturgy is formational, there's more to formation than passing on information. Here are some "right-brain" considerations for children's liturgies:

1) People who love each other show it to children not merely in words but by making signs of love to each other.

2) Liturgy should involve body, mind, senses, imagination, emotions, memory (cf. *Environment and Art in Catholic Worship*, #5).

3) *How* we do things is as important as *what* we do at liturgy.

4) The non-verbal communicates as powerfully as the verbal.

5) Children will be as affected by the environment and music as by the spoken word.

Symbol, Story, Space

Some food (snacks?) for thought for liturgical ministers preparing liturgies at which children are present:

Environment. If there is a separate space for the children's Liturgy of the Word, what does it look like? Is it an attractive place to spend time? I experienced a liturgy for children that took place in a cafeteria with few windows, no art, and although it smelled a little like peanut butter, it did not seem to help call me to an awareness that the Mass is a meal. Children will remember their worship space just as we remember ours from our childhood. Make it beautiful.

Symbols. Are our children familiar with the basic symbols of our faith — such as fire, water, bread, wine, oil, assembly, table, book? Butterflies, empty tombs, flowers, banners, and the like are all variations on the original. Teach the original. As we musicians know, you can't enjoy the variation unless you've first been given the theme.

Sense of Sacred. Do our children have a sense of reverence for our sacred symbols? Do we light candles ceremoniously, or do we flick Bics? Do we treat the altar as a holy table or as a bulletin board where we hang things that the children (or anybody) have created? Do we treat objects with more reverence than we treat one another?

Story. Are we telling the whole story to the children? Do they know our traditions? Are we providing them with the whole story musically? Are they familiar with hymns and psalms as well as with contemporary musical texts? Do they hear classical religious music as well as Christian rock? Do they know of God's strength as well as God's gentleness?

Psalms and Children

We sing psalms at liturgy for several reasons. 1) Their texts are from the bible and should last a lifetime. 2) We pray the psalms because Jesus prayed the psalms. 3) The psalms express a wide range of human emotions — something very important to the life of the soul.

We all remember the music of our childhood. Many even remember all the words from the devotional hymns they learned as children. Practically every cradle Catholic over the age of 35 can sing hymns like "Holy God, We Praise Thy Name" by heart. People learned this text when they were young children. So why don't we give the kids the best of what musical/liturgical texts have to offer? The psalms, for example. Parents and children could sing and pray them together and pass them on to their children's children if someone would take the time to catechize the parents and teach the songs to children of all ages (as well as aging children).

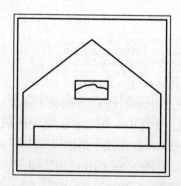

Of Christmas Past and Present

It is becoming popular in many parishes to celebrate the Christmas liturgy with children in mind. I know of one parish that has two evening Masses, one at 5:30 and one at 7:30. Many parents like to take their children to Mass on Christmas Eve. Naturally, the parents with younger children come to the earlier Mass. As a result the Masses are slightly different (and so is the noise level).

In some places, the entertainment model reigns. By this I mean children's pageants, a live nativity scene during the gospel, or Santa Claus as the grand finale. Now, really! Is this what it's all about? On an occasion as significant in the lives of children as Christmas, planners must remember that the liturgy itself will carry the celebration. Planners should be super-prepared. The liturgy need not be longer than usual. Nor should it be burdened with extras. It should be efficient yet not hurried. No commentaries are needed. Homilies should be brief and to the point.

Tradition is very important on a night like this. Simple traditional Christmas carols are the order of the evening. It is probably more important to teach kids the traditional carols than to sing children's ditties with them. When and how did you learn the words and tunes of the traditional carols? You probably sang them in church as a child. Or you sang them at home. These traditional songs carry memory with them throughout our lives. Each time we sing them we remember our story. They bring us comfort. They connect us with other generations, other faiths, other cultures.

Let's not cheat our children of the richness of tradition. The future church will be determined by the seeds that we are planting now.

7

Rites and Sacraments

Baptism

Know the Rite!

The *Rite of Baptism for Children* (RBC) consists of a introduction and seven chapters. Never skip over the introduction when you read a rite. Much can be gleaned from it. The first three chapters of the document pertain to numbers of children being baptized. Chapter I concerns baptism of several children; Chapter II, one child; Chapter III, a large number of children. The next two chapters concern the ministers. Chapter IV is for times when the sacrament is administered by a catechist when no priest or deacon is available. Chapter V covers baptism for children in danger of death when no priest or deacon is available. Chapter VI discusses bringing a baptized child into the church. (Obviously there is no pouring of water again, but after the litany the child is anointed and given the baptismal garment and the lighted candle.) Chapter VII suggests various texts for use in the celebration of baptism for children.

Besides recommending scripture readings and alternative general intercessions, Chapter VII includes recommended responsorial psalms: Psalm 23 ("The Lord is My Shepherd"); Psalm 27 ("The Lord is My Light and Salvation"); Psalm 34 (you may know this either as "Taste and See" [verse 9] or "Come to Me" [verse 6]).

The rites of the church are available in paperback and study editions. Liturgy committees should familiarize themselves with all of these documents.

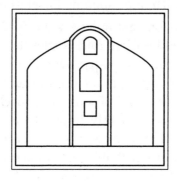

Infant Baptism

I have asked my friend Paul Covino to do the impossible and say *only* a few words about infant baptism. Here is his response.

The *Rite of Baptism for Children* (RBC) contains several key principles to guide parish celebrations of infant baptism:

1) The faith of the church is expressed through the participation of parishioners in the baptismal liturgy. The rite envisions infant baptism as *normally* being celebrated communally, with parishioners present and all the recently born babies baptized at one liturgy (see Chapter I, RBC).

2) Since baptism is initiation into the Paschal Mystery, it is best celebrated at times of Paschal significance. Easter, Pentecost, the Baptism of the Lord, and All Saints Day are obvious opportunities. Depending on the number of babies baptized in the parish each year, additional Sundays in Ordinary Time could be identified by reviewing the Lectionary for readings with baptismal or Paschal references.

3) Immersion (not submersion) is the more complete symbol of baptism and is therefore preferred to "infusion" or pouring water over the baby's head. A permanent font suitable for the immersion of infants and adults is the goal of current church documents. Most infants are perfectly happy to be immersed in warm water; they are used to this from bathtime. More often than not, babies cry at baptisms because the water runs into their eyes with infusion.

Paul's M.A. in liturgical research and his thesis on infant baptism have given him much insight, but being the father of four young boys has given him more pastoral and practical wisdom than any book. Thanks, Paul.

Scheduling Infant Baptisms

How do you schedule occasions for infant baptism at parish liturgies? First, look at the readings. If you schedule baptisms on the basis of the Lectionary, be sure to rotate the Masses at which they take place. Everybody gets tired of having baptisms too often at the same Mass.

A possible solution? Example: One week a parish celebrated baptism at the 4:30 P.M. Saturday evening vigil and at 10:00 A.M. Sunday. The next week it celebrated baptism at 8:45 A.M. and 12:30 P.M. Sunday. It did not celebrate baptism the following week.

By the way, it is perfectly acceptable to baptize at vigil Masses on Saturday evenings. Why should we deprive certain parishioners of the experience of this sacrament just because they attend a vigil Mass? A baptism has special meaning for members of a particular assembly if a baby's family participates with it regularly. Those members probably had some awareness of the pregnancy. What joy they experience as they welcome that new member! Isn't the church about relationships? In large parishes, relationships are enormously hard to establish. And certainly, baptism should take place where children participate. A child can remember a baptism vividly for life.

Baptisms During Mass

We are told in RBC (#9) that "the sacrament may be celebrated during Mass, so that the entire community may be present and the relationship between baptism and eucharist may be clearly seen." Again, be sure that these baptisms do not happen too often at the same liturgy.

When the idea of celebrating baptism during Mass comes up, the time factor can sometimes be a major concern. It would be helpful for liturgy committees and pastors to study the rite carefully. When baptism procedures are well-rehearsed, a team of people helps with the ceremonies, and the musicians know what they're doing, the liturgy is not inappropriately long. Most people complain about how long it takes because so often it is done inefficiently. It can actually *seem* longer than it is.

Making Baptisms Run Smoothly

The introductory rites, as liturgists remind us, are cumbersome. Add the sacrament of baptism, its reception, etc., and things could get really tedious. Keep in mind that when baptism is celebrated during Mass, the introductory rites will include the reception of the baptismal parties, the affirmation of the people to raise the children in the Catholic faith, the signing of the cross on the children's foreheads by the presider, parents, and godparents, and a song to process to the place where the Liturgy of the Word will be proclaimed.

Here's one way to incorporate baptism into the introductory rites. The liturgy could begin at the entrance to the worship space with the baptismal parties already in place. If necessary, an introduction by someone in the sanctuary area would call the assembly together, and then the focus would shift to the place where the families are gathered and the affirmation takes place. As the children are signed, why not involve the entire assembly by asking all parents to sign their children with the sign of the cross? This can be followed by the Gloria as the procession moves to the front of the church. (Remember: There is no penitential rite.)

Introductory rites can flow gracefully and simply from the reception at the door of the church through the gathering song to the opening prayer. If we prepare thoughtfully, baptisms need not lengthen the liturgy unduly.

But give the priest a break. He may have had to celebrate several Masses that day. Remind him of procedures for this Mass before the liturgy begins and take a minute to talk through any adaptations.

More Than Pouring Water

When baptism is celebrated during Sunday Mass, musicians need to take care that baptismal music does not dominate the entire eucharistic celebration. There's no need to sing water songs throughout the Mass. We've all done it at some time in our careers, haven't we? Does this look familiar from your old planning sheets? The entrance song was "Come to the Water," the psalm — Psalm 23 with the "beside the waters" verse, "Flow, River, Flow" was used during the presentation of the gifts, and "As the Deer Longs for Running Streams" at communion.

Alas! I know I'm guilty. But not anymore. Now I know that I can use music that has broader range of topics because I've looked at the *Rite of Baptism*. There are other aspects to the rite besides water. At communion time sing music appropriate to the rite of receiving communion, not songs about coming to the water. Songs with texts like one Lord, one faith, one baptism; wake from your sleep; I am the light of the world; church of God, chosen people — led out of darkness — into his marvelous light; amazing grace; God is love; you are God's work of art; walk in his love . . . There's just so much more suitable music available now.

Each Sunday also has its own readings that evoke musical selections, even when there's a baptism. Choose music that highlights baptism and works well throughout the year whenever an assembly celebrates baptism. Select acclamations that can become customary for parish baptisms, and commit them to memory.

Some "Welcome" Help for Masses with Baptisms

Here are some words that might help with the welcome on days of baptism. It may require modification for your situation.

Parents with infants, godparents, presbyters, readers, altar ministers, and hospitality ministers gather at the entry. The reader or the leader of song goes to the ambo and says:

Good morning. On behalf of all parishioners,
I would like to welcome guests and visitors to
_____Church today, especially the
relatives and friends of the *(names of the baptism
families)* _____ families. Today
the whole parish celebrates because this is the day
that *(names of children to be baptized)* _____
_____ will be baptized into the faith of Christ.

So that there are no strangers in our midst,
let us turn now and greet one another. *(Pause
a few moments; then continue.)*

Please remain seated and turn toward the entry
(point) where our liturgy will continue.

Penance

Where to Begin

The first step in understanding the rite of penance is to get a copy of the rite itself. Too often discussions of this sort revolve around a preconceived notion of the rite (often based on our own childhood experiences) or on what we would like to see happen.

The *Rite of Penance* is divided into four chapters and three appendices. Chapter I is the Rite of Reconciliation of Individual Penitents. Chapter II is the Rite of Reconciliation of Several Penitents with Individual Confession and Absolution. Chapter III contains the Rite of Reconciliation of Several Penitents with General Confession and Absolution. Chapter IV contains greetings, opening prayers, and scripture texts helpful to the priest for the celebration of the sacrament of reconciliation for one or several penitents. Appendix I contains the formulae for dispensation from "sins now reserved either in themselves or by reason of a censure." Appendix II will be most helpful for us liturgical ministers because it contains sample penitential services for a variety of occasions. Appendix III contains a form of examination of conscience.

For those of you who got excited about the words "general absolution," calm down. It's not what you think. According to the Introduction to the *Rite* (#31), individual, integral confession and absolution remain the only ordinary way for the faithful to reconcile themselves with God and the Church, unless physical or moral impossibility excuses from this kind of confession. Some of the exceptions would be cases involving danger of death or grave need, i.e., not having sufficient confessors available (especially in mission territory). The decision concerning the lawfulness of giving general absolution is reserved to the bishop of the diocese. In places where there is a shortage of priests, a ministry of acceptance and forgiveness by the community can be of great value until Father gets there to give the church's absolution.

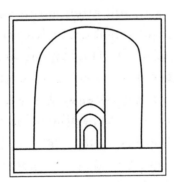

Ritualizing Repentance

A person takes part in a ritual in order to make a public demonstration of something that has already taken place in the person's heart. People seek the sacrament of reconciliation after becoming aware of the alienation in their lives and recognizing the need for healing. The Introduction to the *Rite of Penance* tells us (#2) that the church "possesses both water and tears: the water of baptism, the tears of penance." We are told further that it is the Holy Spirit who moves a person to come to the sacrament of reconciliation.

One of our great privileges and tasks as a priestly people is to listen to one another's stories, to share the burdens, to allow people to reveal the things that haunt and disturb them — to be Christ for one another. When one of us takes the time to listen with full attention to another's story and receives it without judgment and with acceptance, then we act as instruments of the Holy Spirit and instruments of God's grace. The person who is "confessing" — telling his or her own story — is ritualizing the desire to live a new life of liberation from guilt and sin. Without intending to diminish the role of the ordained minister in the sacrament of penance, I would like to suggest that our ordained ministers consider empowering some gifted lay people to facilitate a ministry of reconciliation, to prepare people for the ritual of the sacrament of penance.

Reconciliation as an Ongoing Process

Look at Appendix II of the *Rite of Penance* for sample penance services. There are sample services for Lent, Advent, common penitential celebrations, services for young people, and for the sick. Penance services can be ways of continuing people's reconciliation spirituality. They help to reinforce a person's ongoing struggle with sin, addictions, and attempts to lead a new way of life after an initial conversion experience.

Appendix III contains formulae for an examination of conscience. This section is one of the most pertinent in light of what the church has in common with the very popular twelve-step programs such as Alcoholics Anonymous. It is very interesting how many of the questions are similar to those faced in the twelve steps. (Seems like the church had the idea first, though.) This examination is too complicated to simply be recited during a penance service followed by confession and absolution. What this appendix gives us is the core of an ongoing parish program of reconciliation.

Liturgy committees! How about looking into this?

A Celebration of Reconciliation

For the record, the *Rite of Penance* recommends specific responsorial psalms. They are: Psalms 13, 25, 31, 32, 36, 50, 51, 73, 90, 95, 119, 123, 130, 139, and 143.

Music is an important element of any communal rite. The *Rite of Penance* is no exception. Let's look at Chapter II, an Outline of a Service of Reconciliation with Individual Confession and Absolution. Remember: Not every penitential celebration will have confession and absolution. What we are looking at here is the service *with* absolution, the sacrament of penance.

Introductory Rites. The opening song is followed by a greeting, then an introduction by the priest or another minister to explain the importance and purpose of the celebration and the order of service (I hope the need for this will be eliminated as people become more familiar with the rite). This is followed by the opening prayer.

Celebration of the Word of God. This can be like the usual Liturgy of the Word that people are familiar with from Sunday — reading, psalm, silence, second reading, gospel acclamation and gospel, and homily. For pastoral reasons this section may be shortened to just one reading. But if only one reading is used, it should be a gospel reading. An examination of conscience follows the homily.

Rite of Reconciliation. This begins with a general confession of sins, that is, a communal formula such as the Confiteor, followed by a litany or a song. The litany may be sung. The examples suggest a penitential litany with the response, "We pray you, hear us" or "Lord, have mercy." This is followed by the Lord's prayer. At this point, individual confession and absolution take place. After confessions are over, a hymn or psalm in acknowledgment of God's power and mercy is sung. The rite gives the Canticle of Mary and Psalm 136 as examples. The closing prayer is followed by the blessing and dismissal.

Eucharist/First Communion

Different Strokes . . .

Some children receive first communion with their class and others receive with their families. There are good reasons for both approaches.

If the children are receiving first eucharist with their classmates, may I suggest a few tips to reduce your headaches and symptoms of burnout?

The music for first eucharist should be primarily the music of the celebrating community, some of which should already be familiar to the children if they attend Sunday Mass. This means that the music will be, for the most part, music chosen from the parish repertoire from Sunday eucharist. I am, of course, presuming that the assemblies at Sunday Masses are singing some common repertoire — at least the acclamations and responses. After all, it is mostly the parents and the family members who will and should be doing much of the singing at first eucharist.

This is also true for those receiving the sacrament of confirmation. The tortuous rehearsals that musicians put teenagers through in the name of preparation for confirmation would be eliminated by using this approach.

Make life easier for yourself. Tell your catechists and religious education specialists about this.

First Communion with Families — Go for It

For those parishes who are considering integrating their reception of first eucharist into the Sunday liturgies, I urge you to hold on to this dream! Don't give up the possibility of making it work! It can happen if you want it to. What a wonderful experience for a child to be able to receive first communion along with his or her family, and not just have the families watching from the side pews. What a powerful image of eucharist: the child surrounded by family and encircled by the communion of saints.

If your parish is large, the logistics need a lot of thought. You may be able to have the best of both worlds by dividing the class into smaller groups. Some churches can't hold the large crowds that first communion involves. Breaking into smaller groups could actually help solve this problem.

Don't give up the idea. It's worth the effort it takes to make it work.

First Communion within Sunday Masses

There are ways to foster the idea of celebrating first communion at Sunday liturgies. Begin the process by allowing families to choose it as an option. Children could choose to receive first communion with their families during Sunday Masses from Easter to Pentecost rather than in the "traditional" large group situation. Get the minister of religious education to agree to have the children's education completed by Easter. There are a decent number of Sundays — including Easter and Pentecost — available for first communion (plus the Feast of the Ascension if you want). If you're going to consider moving in this direction, plan a year in advance.

Draw up a list of available Masses — vigil Masses too. Families may then sign up. (Another model is for small groups/classes to sign up.) On the day of the event, reserve the necessary rows of seats near the altar area for the first communicants and their families. Just before liturgy, the first communicants can be brought to the presider to be greeted and then lined up in the entrance procession. As the procession passes the family pew, the child "peels off" and joins the family. They could sit at the end of the pews so as to be seen. The presider might mention the name of the child or children receiving first eucharist that day in his opening remarks at the greeting or in the general intercessions. The child or children may be invited to stand next to the presider at the altar during the eucharistic prayer. At the sign of peace, the child returns to the family. The family then comes forward together with the child to receive eucharist. Ushers hold communion distribution until this moment passes.

Of course, all this has hitches and glitches. But it can be done, and the long-term results will be most rewarding!

Sacramental Preparation —
Not for Children Only

Preparation for first communion (and first penance) is an excellent time to catechize parents. Remember: If you want to get through to the children, you'll have to work on the parents. Those kids who got caught in the undertow of Vatican II renewal twenty years ago are now the parents of those seven-year-olds who are making their first communions this year.

Those very parents need not only an understanding of liturgy, but a sense of ritual as well. How many families today actually take the time to dine together? Not just eat together, but dine? The microwave has added new meaning to the term "fast food."

It would be helpful to have parents and children experience a ritual meal together. This can be done within the sacramental preparation program by inviting them all to a formal dinner. Potluck is fine. Dress-up is essential. Some children might design and make (paint, color, print) the invitations. Others might make place cards and name tags. Some might plan the dinner music. Some might even make candles. Parents might be asked to bring a candle (3" in diameter x 6" long) to light and to rekindle at home as a remembrance of the event. Some children could make the dinner rolls. Don't forget the grape juice (wine for adults?).

How about an environment committee for the dinner? Flowers? Banners? Family photos? Family trees? You might want the children to grow some plants for the room that can be given to parents as a memento.

Procure the music and the audiotape of a table prayer such as "God of Life and of the Living" by Michael Joncas. Table prayers have elements of eucharistic prayers but can function well as "grace before meals." They can be modified to fit the needs of the group. In Joncas' version, two cantors — one male, one female — lead the prayer, which includes an attractive easy assembly part (hymn cards are available). Cantor parts may be adapted somewhat for recitation where necessary. Let the children listen to the tape of the table prayer as they work on their projects for the dinner. Bread is broken and passed around, and juice (or wine) is poured as the table prayer music comes to an end. Then everyone sits down to dine. This is a great way to teach eucharist. It may even help people remember their facts better.

Sound like a lot of work? It is, but if children are working in small groups, you could probably talk with them about eucharist as you work together. They're capable of doing both simultaneously. (The question is whether or not the teacher can handle it.)

First Communion: Something for All of Us

In the past, first communion focused only on the recipients of the sacrament. But imagine how many people might be affected by this symbol of our living faith if it took place regularly within the Sunday liturgy.

A parishioner once told me that after experiencing a Sunday Mass at which first eucharist was celebrated, he kept thinking of his own children's first communion years before. He was inspired enough to talk with his grown children (who weren't regular churchgoers) about the importance of passing on the faith to his grandchildren. Perhaps someone participating in this celebration will remember a time of closeness between parent and child who are now alienated. Perhaps reconciliation will follow. I believe this is the presence of the Holy Spirit at liturgy . . . moving through us all . . . to help and heal us. It is our privilege to cooperate with the Holy Spirit.

Here are few tips for celebrating first communion with children.

1) Use the sprinkling rite to call to mind the children's baptism. Do this at the introductory rites. Or, renew baptismal vows after the homily and sprinkle the assembly then.

2) Get parents involved with the readings. If children proclaim the word, let the parent escort the

child to the ambo and stand beside or near the child during the reading. The child is perfectly capable of reading without assistance. This is not the point. Some important non-verbal proclamation is happening as well. The symbol of parent and child together says to the assembly that sharing the word is something families do together. It also gives a sign that the role of the parent *as minister* is one of presence as well as function. Liturgy is not for children only. Children grow into liturgy through the example of their families. Let symbols speak. Affirm the importance of the parents in the religious formation of children. In my neighborhood, parents are religious about attending and supporting their children's soccer games and various sports activities. Is it possible for us to help call attention to the importance of their presence in the liturgical life of the kids, too?

More Suggestions for First Communion

Here are some suggestions for celebrating first communion apart from the Sunday liturgies. Several of them can also be applied to reception of confirmation.

· Parents are the primary caretakers of the religious formation of their children. Pray for and acknowledge the parents in the general intercessions before teachers and others are mentioned.

· Sometimes because of all the hard work that goes into a celebration of this sort, there can be a tendency to use the general intercessions as a place for special "thank you's." Not! Acknowledgments can be made at the announcement time, after the final prayer, or in the program.

· Before dismissal, ask parents to rise. Bless them as the primary caretakers of the religious formation of their children. Consider teaching the children to extend their hands to bless the parents.

· When printing a program for the children, remember that young children cannot read music. Memorize. Use music familiar to the entire community.

· One parish asked children to do artwork in the program. Small biblical pictures sketched by kids were photocopied onto the program. Might children color worship programs?

· If the kids wear special clothes for first communion during the Great Fifty Days, encourage them to wear them each Sunday till Pentecost. It is not unusual in various cultures for people to cherish the clothing and accoutrements from sacred and important celebrations of their lives. What one wears is not necessarily a question of materialism. It can be an attempt to create a tangible memory of a spiritual experience.

Weddings

But It's My Wedding . . .

People are always asking questions about music for weddings. Since it's so important to so many people, let's start at the beginning. First, the *Constitution on the Sacred Liturgy* calls liturgy "the worship of the divine majesty" (CSL #33). Because a Catholic wedding is liturgy, the music should help the assembly give thanks and praise to God. So should all the other components, including the readings. Liturgy "contains rich instruction for the faithful" (CSL #33). God speaks to the chosen people in liturgy. The words of Kahlil Gibran (or any other popular writer) do not "stand in" for God's words.

Second, the wedding liturgy is a celebration of the universal church. The particular community of faith is the assembly of family, friends, and other parishioners. In some cultures, weddings have long taken place at the Sunday parish eucharist.

Third, since liturgy is the public worship of God, shouldn't wedding music serve the assembly that they might worship? Shouldn't music help the members thank God for bringing this couple together? If we answer yes, then our job is to help the assembly participate more fully in the liturgy through music. It follows that wedding music should be music of the assembly, not just favorite songs of a bride or a groom. The texts need to be solid, the melodies singable, and the style suitable to the day and to the people who are at prayer.

Are All Weddings the Same?

We have three forms of the wedding rite in Roman Catholicism: 1) The rite during Mass; 2) The rite outside Mass; 3) The rite between a Roman Catholic and an unbaptized person.

Second, we distinguish among the various parts of each form. Each of the three forms has a) gathering and entrance rites, b) Liturgy of the Word, c) marriage rite, and d) concluding rites. Form 1, which is recommended for a marriage between two Catholics, adds the eucharistic liturgy and the communion rite between the marriage rite and the concluding rites. Musically, all three forms may have a gathering song, responsorial psalm, and gospel acclamation. There may be a song within the marriage rite, and there may be a hymn of thanksgiving during the concluding rites. If the eucharist is celebrated, there may be instrumental music, a choral setting, a solo, a song by the assembly, or silence during the preparation of the gifts. Eucharistic acclamations are recommended. Music ministers have to know the assembly in order to choose music that all can sing.

A Song Leader Can Help . . .

People are so funny at weddings. Don't you just love to watch them? Can you distinguish the people who haven't been to church in years from the non-Catholics? It's easy. Neither the Catholics nor the non-Catholics seem to know when to sit or stand. The Catholics act like they've never been to Mass before, but you know they have because when they enter they genuflect and bless themselves with the sign of the cross. But sing? No way. Participate? Nada. They come to watch now and party later.

Well, it's time to get these weddings into shape. And the first person you will need to help you is a knowledgeable song leader. If someone's relative wants to sing, fine. Let her or him perform the solo while the mother of the bride or groom is being seated or as guests find places. The soloist may sing during the preparation of the gifts or after the communion song of the assembly. It is possible for the soloist to learn the responsorial psalm or communion song, but the assembly should join her or him antiphonally. And communication with the assembly is essential — a wedding needs someone who knows how to talk with the assembly and engage them in active participation, not merely sing for them. It is a skill. Not everyone's singing relatives have this skill. (Also don't presume that every couple who mentions that there is someone in the family who sings necessarily *wants* that person to sing. Sometimes the relative offers, and the bride or groom doesn't want to hurt the person's feelings.

A question such as, "Have you heard this person sing?" "Is this person trained to lead music at liturgy?" may help take the couple off the hook.)

What about the expense of using a parish cantor or leader of song when one might use a relative, even if the relative is not trained? Compared to money spent on flowers alone, for example, music fees are a small price to pay for professionally-done liturgical music for weddings. What will people remember months later? What would be missed most at a wedding? Flowers or music? Musicians need to take themselves seriously when it comes to weddings. It is an opportunity for reconciliation among relatives, a return to church for some folks who no longer attend, and a renewal of commitment and love for all.

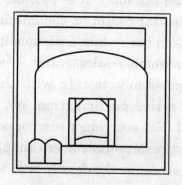

Active Participation at Weddings

At weddings, there are people who cannot wait for the church ceremony to be over so that the celebration might begin. But the celebration begins *with* the wedding ceremony, not afterward. How can we fan the flames of a celebrative spirit within the assembly at weddings? How can we minimize their passive-spectator attitude?

Getting off to a great start at a wedding liturgy can make quite a difference. And weddings have great starts already built in. The movement of the procession at a wedding liturgy powerfully and dramatically symbolizes passage to new life. It evokes awe and sometimes even moves us to tears. People are already filled with emotion — they will certainly have something to express after witnessing so beautiful a beginning. So how can we capture the acclamation of the assembly at this time?

Try this: After the procession, the presider, another minister, or the couple addresses the assembly in words like these: "Today is a very special day for us [or for *N.* and *N.*]. Two lives are joined together and two families become one. In order to celebrate this unity, let everyone turn and meet and greet one another." After the greeting, the presider may say, "Let us praise God for life and love on this day by singing our gathering song." Trust me. They will sing. Gathering people well can work wonders.

Why Aren't They Singing?

If you are still trying to get people to sing as the bridal party comes down the aisle, good luck. I don't think it's going to happen. After all, the words on the page of a songbook are competing here with beautiful people dressed in their best for the occasion of a lifetime. And if you're still hiring soloists instead of song leaders, you'd better read on.

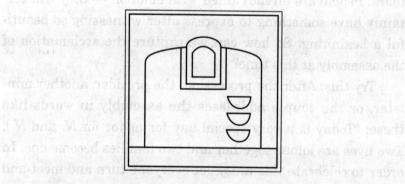

What Shall We Sing?

The music for the wedding should be liturgical, not devotional. What is the difference between devotion and liturgy? Devotions "are religious exercises (prayers, methods of meditation, orders of service, rituals, gestures) whose texts and rubrics are not contained in the official liturgical books of the Roman rite" (Carl Dehne, SJ, *The New Dictionary of Sacramental Worship*). Devotions include exposition and benediction of the Blessed Sacrament, rosary, stations of the cross, novenas, and first Friday devotions. Devotions should "harmonize with the liturgical seasons, accord with the sacred liturgy, are in some way derived from it, and lead the people to it, since, in fact, the liturgy, by its very nature far surpasses any of them" (CSL #13). Liturgy requires an assembly and includes sacraments, divine office, and blessings.

The most appropriate texts for liturgical music are from the Sacramentary or Lectionary. This is true for all liturgical celebrations. Texts that clearly meet the needs of the marriage rite and the criteria for good liturgical language are the psalms of that rite. The responsorial psalms for weddings include Psalms 33, 34, 103, 112, 128, 145, and 148. Other psalms may be sung at the responsorial, and these psalms may be sung elsewhere as well. Other texts may be sung, too. Good liturgical texts contain words of praise and thanksgiving to God. Through them the assembly addresses God. A devotional text, however, is often addressed to a saint. This is why some old favorite hymns simply are not sung in church anymore. They are not the servant of liturgy.

Repertoire for the Assembly

Let's look at a basic repertoire that a heterogeneous assembly can sing together for weddings.

Gathering songs for weddings between Roman Catholics and other Christians (that may be common to both traditions): "Morning Has Broken"; "This Day God Gives Me" (same tune as "Morning Has Broken"); "All Creatures Of Our God And King"; "Alleluia! Sing To Jesus"; "Love Divine, All Loves Excelling" (same tune as "Alleluia! Sing To Jesus"); "Joyful, Joyful, We Adore Thee"; "Praise The Lord, Ye Heavens" (same tune as "Joyful, Joyful"); "Praise God From Whom All Blessings Flow"; "All People That On Earth Do Dwell" (same tune as "Praise God From Whom All Blessings Flow"); "In Christ There Is No East Or West"; "For The Beauty Of The Earth" (especially verse 3 about human love). Some of these would also work as concluding songs. "Now Thank We All Our God" suits the concluding rite as well.

One of the most popular gospel acclamations is the "Celtic Alleluia." Even if the assembly is not familiar with it, members will quickly be able to echo it. It's such a joyful tune for the occasion.

Some couples think that if there is no Mass, the ceremony will consist simply of the marriage vows. Some are unaware that a Catholic wedding always includes a Liturgy of the Word. Yes, even if there is "no Mass," there is still a proclamation of the gospel and a sung Alleluia. It is no longer a 15-minute ceremony. Music is encouraged for the responsorial psalm and the gospel acclamation. There is room for more psalms during the Liturgy of the Word if the couple and the presider desire.

For music with texts geared to wedding liturgies but not to Sunday liturgies, see "Hear Us Now, Our God And Father" for gathering or recessional. "United As One" may be sung by a cantor, with the assembly joining in with "Alleluia." During the preparation of gifts, "Love Which Never Ends" may be sung or, if resources are sparse, the refrain may be sung and the verses recited.

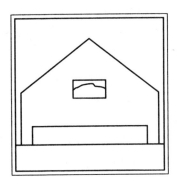

More Repertoire

Some contemporary liturgical gathering songs that may be used at weddings are: "Glory And Praise To Our God"; "Sing A New Song"; and "Lift Up Your Hearts." Some of these suit the dismissal as well. Consider "Canticle Of The Sun" and the less well known but fitting and strong, "Sing Of The Lord's Goodness." For the season of Christmas and Epiphany, two good choices are "Songs Of Thankfulness And Praise" (especially verse two) and "O Come All Ye Faithful."

Music in liturgy is meant to enhance ritual action. For example, the song "Gather Us In" enhances the rite of gathering, as "Come To the Water" enhances the rite of baptism. The song "Taste And See" works both as a responsorial psalm and a communion song, but it would not enhance the rite of baptism. Psalms 16, 23, 84, and 100 are fitting as communion songs especially because members of the assembly can better sing refrains that are strong but not too long.

Besides the psalms, let's look at some other attractive communion songs: "To Be Your Bread Now"; "Everlasting Your Love"; "One Bread, One Body"; "Bread Of Life"; "Eat This Bread"; "Song Of The Body Of Christ"; "How Great Thou Art"; "Love Which Never Ends." Consider *"Pan De Vida"*; *"Envía Tu Espíritu"*; *"Cordero De Dios"*; and the acclamations of *"Misa De Las Américas"* for bilingual assemblies. Instrumental music or silence may be a welcome relief at the preparation of the gifts. There are some communion songs that can work as well for the preparation of the gifts: "Blest Are They"; "Be Not Afraid"; and "Mary's Song" are examples.

How to Help the Couple Make Choices

Wedding music has to be liturgically solid, musically accessible and suitable to the occasion, and fitting for the assembly.

What do I mean, "fitting for the assembly"? I mean, "Does it serve the people who will be there?" The question I ask the couple is not, "What kind of music do you and your families like?" Instead, I ask, "Are you both Roman Catholic? Are your families Roman Catholic? When you go to church do you attend the 'folk' or 'traditional' Mass? Do your families like to sing?" In a marriage between a Roman Catholic and a member of another tradition, I ask both people about their traditions and customs. I try to get a sketch of their faith history. In this way I can help them choose music that connects with their "story," makes for a festive celebration, and fits their style and that of the assembly.

Music for a wedding between a Roman Catholic and an unbaptized person is tricky to plan. Maybe the most common type is that between a Jew and a Catholic. The psalms are always welcome at these weddings. Choose music that is common to both faith traditions and not insensitive. We are not trying to deny what we believe. Rather, we extend hospitality to our guests as Jesus did.

Again, the first meeting sometimes opens doors to a relationship with the couple that lasts a lifetime. I don't mean a relationship with me personally. In a way I am one member of a real flesh-and-blood faith community that we all hope they'll want to become part of, whether here or in another parish. The more parish people they meet, the better. Once they experience a life-giving parish, they won't settle for less. They may have to keep searching until they find a parish that can nourish them and be nourished by them. And isn't that part of what this music ministry is all about?

I know that not all of these suggestions fit everybody. Some parishes don't distinguish between "folk" and "traditional." Some parishes do the whole wedding ministry as a team, with liturgical, financial, pastoral, spiritual, musical, and catechetical input. Hurrah! Someday, in the Holy Spirit, we'll *all* be there! Until then . . .

Close Encounters of the First Kind

When the bride, groom, and I get together for the first meeting, I try to get them to look at the *entire* wedding celebration — not just the liturgy. I usually start by talking about how their love is a gift from God. It's mysterious and wonderful. It's not to be taken for granted. A relationship that blossoms, grows, and points us to a bigger understanding of life, of the world and of God is — well, what else can we call it? — a gift. That gift evokes a hearty "thank you" from us to the Creator.

In the wedding liturgy, we celebrate in a very particular way. We listen to God's word, respond with "alleluia," say "yes," enter a covenant and make a promise, maybe cry a little, remember stories of God's love, hope the couple into the future, rejoice, give thanks, and sing "Amen." When I say things like that, I find that most couples understand and want to celebrate real liturgy as the ritual books suggest.

Reverse Psychology

Sometimes a bride or groom says: "My friend got married in Saint Whomever's Church and didn't have any music, so why do I have to have this?" My answer is: "We're not trying to force you to do something. We try to help you celebrate this love with as much beauty and thanksgiving as possible. We want it to be better than weddings at City Hall where there's no music at all." Reverse psychology can help. After all, we offer them a terrific gift. We're not wedding wardens.

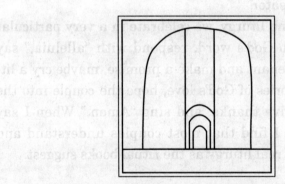

An Audiotape

Couples still don't know much church music. I used to sit down and play through some music for each couple, but I soon ran out of time. Here are some alternatives:

1) Your music catechesis and planning could be a part of the larger parish marriage preparation program. One meeting in that program could address liturgical nuts and bolts.

2) If this cannot happen — for example, if your parish doesn't have a marriage prep — then you could set up a wedding planning evening once a month or once every few months. Bring all the couples together for a music demonstration.

3) You could make an audiotape of processionals, recessionals, psalms, hymns, and acclamations. (This has really helped me.) At least it frames our musical conversation. Help couples choose music that best expresses their faith, taste, and values.

An audiotape that helps couples plan wedding music need not be complex. In making the tape, though, be sure to include a variety of musical styles for both sung and instrumental choices. One or two samples call others to mind. If several parish music ministers work with weddings, why couldn't they all get together to make one tape? If you have budget problems, do what I did. Lease out the audiotape. Have couples pay a $5.00 deposit on it. When they bring it back, the money is returned. It works.

Celebrating Marriage: The Book

I have another suggestion that can lighten your burden. It is a book, *Celebrating Marriage, Preparing the Wedding Liturgy: A Workbook for Engaged Couples,* edited by Paul Covino. Paul offers excellent ritual suggestions, Lawrence Madden discusses Lectionary and homiletic options, John Buscemi addresses the issues of art and environment, and I treat the "why" and "what" questions about wedding music. I think you will find it helpful. Some parishes give copies of this book to engaged couples. If you have a limited budget, use the lease method, as with the audiotapes.

These two items — the audiotape and the book — help me with large numbers of weddings. They save time that I can use more effectively with the couples (listening to their stories, for example).

Don't underestimate the Holy Spirit's power in the liturgy. We all know times when the families at the wedding didn't like each other. And the right music really helped. It made a difference. To make itself heard, the word of God often takes time and energy . . . sometimes yours.

You Want *What* . . . ?

How do I respond when the bride wants "Here Comes the Bride"? I have some creative ways to solve this problem. The first is called the "break-out-in-a-cold-sweat" technique. Put your fingers up to your mouth, start chewing on a fingernail, and try to look like you're thinking really hard. Then say, "Gosh, we don't get many requests for that anymore. It's not really so popular." The bride may then beg you to tell her what's "hot" for processionals nowadays. You then suggest the "Trumpet Tune" and "Voluntary" (Clarke/Purcell) and casually mention that these were used at the wedding of Prince Charles and Lady Diana (of happy memory).

That should do it! If it doesn't, try the "oh-how-tacky" technique. When the bride mentions the Wagner, you simply look shocked and say: "Oh, you mean the one they use on that TV show, *The Dating Game*? And that they've trivialized so on the soap operas? You want *that* at your wedding?" That should seal the deal. For some, however, you may want to use the "liberation" technique. Say, " 'Here Comes the Bride' is sexist. It's the groom's day too, you know." (This always works with the "liturgically correct" crowd.)

Those who simply must have a favorite but inappropriate song can schedule it during the seating of the bride's mother. Guidelines for weddings are the same as for Sunday Mass. No hymns to Mary during communion. Psalms are to be psalms, not favorite songs. Most of the music is to be sung by the assembly.

Be Pastoral . . . It's Not Their Fault

Let's get real here. Some people preparing for marriage haven't set foot in a church for years. They may have dropped out along the way. This time of wedding preparation might lead them to reconciliation with the church. Weddings can be a time of renewal. So the first meeting of a music minister with an engaged couple is key. It must be pastoral and may involve catechesis.

If one of the partners belongs to no particular religious tradition, he or she may find this preparation an enriching introduction to our faith, an opportunity for learning. For others, especially if one partner belongs to another religious tradition, marriage preparation can initiate conversation about and appreciation of our faith. Don't push a couple into a list of "dos" and "don'ts" for weddings. We need policies. But issues far bigger than "Here Comes the Bride" are at stake here.

A Protestant bride-to-be told a colleague of mine that she was hurt and confused when she found out that she couldn't have the Wagner and Mendelssohn wedding marches at her Roman Catholic church wedding. She cherished that custom in her own Protestant tradition. Nobody bothered to give her reasons, even though she asked why the music was considered inappropriate. The only answer she got was that it was policy.

Wasn't that great? Her first introduction to the Catholic community was a rejection of a custom that meant much to her. I don't think we can expect her to embrace Roman Catholicism in the near future. Can't we be a little more pastoral?

Most people have had religious experiences. Such experiences are valid, even if they don't meet someone else's standards. For example, just because I don't consider certain music liturgically appropriate doesn't mean someone else can't derive great inspiration from it.

Maybe the reason so many people wanted selections from *Godspell* for their wedding was that that musical made a greater impact on their teen years than church music did. The music was contemporary and the words religious. It expressed their faith. It connected them to a religious experience. It's not their fault.

We should naturally expect brides and grooms to have some values that differ from ours. I find that some brides operate out of a musical and liturgical vacuum. They have ideas about their weddings based on what they saw when they were kids, what they've heard at friends' weddings, or even what their mothers want. Don't blame these brides. If we want to point a finger, we should start with ourselves. We — musicians, educators, and other liturgical ministers — failed to give them a solid musical and liturgical foundation when they were children. But, then again, if we knew then what we know now. . . .

Focus, Please

We've covered a lot of ground in this section on weddings. Remember, *do not choose all the options!* I'm trying to approach the topic of wedding music for people from sea to shining sea, so I've given lots of selections and suggestions. Consider making a list with one or two choices in each category: gathering song, responsorial psalm, recessional, etc. Add one or two choices that are part of *your* parish repertoire that do not appear on my lists. An audiotape of samples helps people make choices, but preparing one takes effort, especially if much variety is needed. These are only suggestions. You make the decisions. You know your people.

Second, when you prepare a tape for couples, use excerpts. People are busy; one tape usually suffices. You may make two different tapes or repertoire lists and then, after an interview with a couple, decide which best fits their needs. Different strokes for different folks.

By the way, one of my friends was lamenting how many phone calls it took her to find a cantor for a wedding that was coming up. Now, I don't know about you, but I do not contact cantors; the bride or groom does that. I'll give the couple some phone numbers, but it's their job to listen to the cantors, choose who they want, and make arrangements. The couple needs this involvement. It is good for them to know the people who lead the singing at the wedding liturgy.

Music ministers handle wedding preparations in different ways. If it ain't broke, don't fix it, as they say. But perhaps some of these ideas can lighten your load. And remember, be pastoral and sensitive.

Funerals

Some Tasks for Liturgy Committees

When I was a high school student, I sometimes played the organ for funerals when I had no idea who was being buried. There was a standard repertoire, vestments were black, and the norm in my neighborhood was a solemn high Mass requiring a priest, deacon, and sub-deacon.

Since those days major transitions have occurred in our Catholic celebrations of the rites surrounding death and dying. Perhaps your liturgy committee could take some time to look at funeral customs and procedures in the parish. Here are some discussion questions:

1) Are funerals recognized as important events in your parish?

2) Does the leadership of the parish respond to the bereaved as well as to the deceased? (For example, does the parish council president, or a delegate, assume a role here?)

3) Does the family of the deceased have to handle the burden of contacting their own musicians, etc.?

4) Does the funeral director have greater responsibility to the bereaved than the parish family does?

5) There are parishes that have Resurrection or Lazarus choirs made up of people who are available to sing for funerals. What does your ministry offer?

We Have to Talk

It is never comfortable to talk about death. But how can we avoid the subject of death if we take resurrection seriously?

We know that matter cannot be destroyed. It changes form. After death our earthly remains, which are ultimately bone fragments and ashes, return to God's universe. But the child of God, who we are, lives on. Can we, then, as Catholic Christians, justify the amount of money spent on elaborate caskets, flowers, limousines, and more, just for putting a dead body to rest (. . . in a style to which most of us were not accustomed in life)? Many funeral directors are more than willing to minister to a truly Christian burial, but they, too, are victims of society's demands to deny the stark reality of death.

The subject of extravagant Christian funeral practices needs attention. Are your parishioners aware of the alternatives to this misdirected outpouring of love for a life well lived? It is encouraging to see the number of families who request donations to charity "in lieu of flowers." It's a start. Do you think people are aware of the less expensive and now permissible cremation alternatives for Catholics? How about willing a body to science or donating organs? (The body can still be present for the funeral Mass.) How about urging people to take control of their own funeral arrangements? (Obviously, this must be done before death — but not in the will, since the will is usually opened after the burial.)

These issues need attention, first of all, from the pulpit. When was the last time you heard a homily about funeral customs and rites? (Ordinarily, I wouldn't suggest the homily as the proper place for catechesis of this kind, but this is an issue that concerns us all, and we need to be educated about it.)

Bereavement Ministries

Musicians (organists, other instrumentalists, and cantors/singers) greatly enrich the funeral liturgy. Music can be a great source of comfort to the mourners. I experienced this myself while visiting a parish where there was a vigil (wake) for a woman who had been murdered. Parish musicians showed up and sang at the vigil. The mourners were in too much pain to sing. But it didn't matter. They were listening intently. I could see the comfort and gratitude in their eyes for the gifts of music and people at this time. They were deeply touched that the musicians cared enough to do this. The musicians transformed the room. This was truly an instance in which music touched places that words could not.

Considering the size of some parishes, or the large number of funerals that take place in some communities, the parish musician cannot be expected to do everything. Here is an opportunity for other capable musicians to give service to the parish. Musicians who cannot serve regularly, or who are in training or perhaps retired, might be able to help out for funeral liturgies. Parishes that have formed Lazarus choirs or Resurrection choirs specifically to serve at funeral Masses need to consider expanding this ministry to include the vigil as well.

And while we're on the subject of ministries and funeral liturgies, let's spend a moment talking about some other ministries to the bereaved. Is there a ministry of bereavement in your parish? Do parishioners look in on the family after the funeral? Could the parish council send a letter of condolence on behalf of the entire parish family at the loss of one of their members? Would it be possible for the ushers/ministers of hospitality to be present to help welcome people at the church? Familiar faces are a great comfort to people at times of bereavement. Why should the undertaker have to handle all these ministries? Ministry is *being present to* people as much as it is *doing things for* people.

A New Document

The *Order of Christian Funerals* (OCF) is one of the most recent liturgical documents to be revised. It consists of a general introduction and five chapters. Part I concerns the vigil (what used to be known as the wake), the funeral liturgy with Mass or outside Mass, and the rite of committal. It also contains a sensitive section called Related Rites and Prayers. This contains prayers for after someone has died, prayers for when gathering in the presence of the body (when the family first sees the body at the wake), and prayers for when the body is transferred to the church or to the cemetery. Part II contains the funeral rites for children. This is similar in format to Part I. Part III is very helpful for liturgy preparation since it contains scripture texts for these liturgies. Part IV is the office for the dead — morning and evening prayer. Part V contains prayers for particular circumstances — death after a lingering illness, suicide, and the death of a young person. This section has been handled with grace and sensitivity.

The Spirit of the Law

The OCF must be commended for its beautiful texts. When reading it, keep in mind that it was prepared for an international community and not just for the American church. Therefore, some things may strike you as unusual. For example, we wear white vestments at funerals to proclaim life over death. But in some cultures, white represents death. (Imagine the confusion when a white garment is used as a baptismal garment on a baby in that culture.) Therefore, you will notice that the new rite says that black vestments are permissible for funerals. This is not a return to the days of the Council of Trent, but an accommodation to cultural differences in an international ritual book. This doesn't justify white suburban presiders in white suburbia, USA, wearing black vestments for old times' sake. Get real. We're not going back to the past on this one!

Christian Symbols

Another interesting feature of the OCF is the placing of Christian symbols on the coffin as the funeral liturgy begins. After the pall (a reminder of the baptismal garment), the book of the gospels or a bible may be placed on the coffin "as a sign that Christians live by the word of God and that fidelity to that word leads to eternal life" (OCF, #38). A cross may also be placed there, though many coffins already have them affixed. The Easter candle is to be in place and not carried in procession.

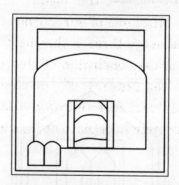

New Vocabulary

We need to become familiar with some new vocabulary. In the OCF, "Funeral Liturgy" refers to two liturgical celebrations only: "Funeral Mass" and "Funeral Liturgy Outside Mass." The latter rite will be extremely helpful for those parishes that are becoming "priest-less." You will notice that the instructions in the Funeral Mass are directed to the priest; whereas the Funeral Liturgy Outside Mass guides the "presiding minister."

What used to be called the "wake" is now called the "vigil." The vigil is stage one of our journey. Stage two is the funeral liturgy, and stage three is the rite of committal. The rite of committal is the conclusion of the funeral rites and may take place at the grave, tomb, or crematorium. If the final commendation and farewell do not take place at the funeral liturgy, they may take place at the rite of committal.

Shaping the Ceremonies

The vigil may take place in the home, in the funeral parlor, or at the church. It may take place in the morning or the evening. It may be a Liturgy of the Word or a form of the office for the dead from the liturgy of the hours (see Part IV: Office for the Dead). Two forms of the vigil are presented in the OCF: "Vigil for the Deceased" and "Vigil for the Deceased with Reception at the Church." The latter means that the "wake" takes place at church. This is already a custom in some churches and dioceses. That which is probably most common is the vigil at the funeral parlor on the night before the Mass and burial. So let's look at that one first.

The structure of the vigil in the form of a Liturgy of the Word consists of the introductory rites (greeting, opening song or hymn, opening prayer); Liturgy of the Word (first reading, responsorial psalm, gospel, short homily); prayer of intercession (litany, Lord's prayer, concluding prayer); and a concluding rite (blessing). Just before the concluding rite, a member or friend of the family may speak in remembrance of the deceased. After the blessing, a gesture (for example, the signing of the forehead of the deceased with a sign of the cross) may take place accompanied with the words, "Eternal rest . . . ." The vigil may conclude in silence or with a song.

Please remember our pastoral responsibilities. If the rosary is part of the tradition at a wake, be sensitive. Recite a decade before or after the vigil service if necessary. These are painful days for people who are grieving. They will want what is familiar to them. Move forward slowly. The greatness of the new ritual is its concern for the mourners.

Liturgy of the Hours and Funerals

The funeral vigil may also be celebrated with some form of the office for the dead. In order to encourage this, Part Four of the OCF provides us with morning prayer and evening prayer. In some places the vigil and the Mass take place in the evening and the burial takes place the next day. In situations such as this, morning prayer can be used before the procession to the place of committal. In other places, the wake and the Mass take place in the morning. Morning prayer can be very beautiful in either situation.

The liturgy of the hours is always most effective when sung. The funeral rite, in fact, encourages singing at these liturgies. "In the choice of music," it says, "preference should be given to the singing of the hymn, the psalmody, and the gospel canticle. [Then] an organist or other instrumentalist and a cantor should assist the assembly in singing the hymn, psalms and responses. The parish community should also prepare booklets or participation aids that contain an outline of the hour, the texts and music belonging to the people, and directions for posture, gesture and movement" (OCF, #372).

If we are going to use the liturgy of the hours, we will have some homework to attend to. If morning prayer or evening prayer is not part of the liturgical life of the parish, either will seem foreign at a vigil. A vigil is not the time to catechize the people. Liturgy of the hours is as much a part of the public worship of the church as is the Mass. How often does it happen at your parish?

Some occasions for the implementation of the liturgy of the hours might be: Advent Vespers; daily morning prayer during Lent; All Souls Day, Nov. 2; celebration of feasts of the saints; an Ash Wednesday service.

The psalmody of morning prayer for the office of the dead consists of Psalm 51 (used on Ash Wednesday and during Lent), Psalms 146 or 150, and an Old Testament canticle from Isaiah. If substitution is necessary, remember that Psalm 51 is a psalm of lament and petition, and the other two are psalms of praise. A New Testament canticle from Luke — the Canticle Of Zachary — is also used. The psalmody of evening prayer consists of Psalm 121 and Psalm 130, both lament psalms, and a New Testament canticle from the letter of Paul to the Philippians. The Canticle of Mary then follows.

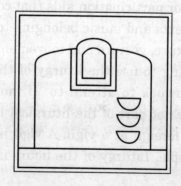

Music for Funerals: Getting It Right

The *Order of Christian Funerals* is *the* sourcebook for Christian funerals. It wonderfully proclaims our Christian theology of death and burial, and will form and inform us as we make liturgical, musical, and pastoral decisions in our parishes. Education and formation will help prevent abuses of our rituals.

Here is just one example of such an abuse, one that I hope will be eliminated by a deeper understanding of the intent of the new rite: More than once at funerals, I have heard Gregory Norbet's "Hosea" used as a responsorial psalm. It is neither a psalm nor an appropriate substitution for a psalm at funerals. The biblical story is about a wife who keeps running away with other men. Hosea's words, "Come back to me," are a statement of his willingness to forgive again and again. It is a significant text about God's continual love for us, even as sinners, but it certainly doesn't express what we Christians believe about death. I've also heard it sung at the commendation and farewell. Now really. Does it make sense at a place in the rite where we are sending off our brother or sister to God in the company of the saints that we should sing "Come back to me"? "Hosea" has a place in worship, but not here.

I won't even mention some of my other horror stories. You have your own, I know! Suffice it to say, the commendation is not the time to perform the deceased's favorite song.

I urge all of you to beg, borrow, or buy a copy of the new rite. Before you purchase commentaries, go to the original text and read it for yourself. There are several editions available and all are beautifully bound.

What Shall We Sing?

From a musical standpoint, some may favor a standardized musical repertoire for funerals. But pastorally, I would recommend the use of appropriate songs and hymns that are used by the community at Sunday liturgies and are also included and recommended in the new rite. Why? Because those songs and hymns that sustain our faith in our lifetime should sustain us through death as well. The task at hand for musicians will be to incorporate the psalms recommended in the new rite into our parish prayer life throughout the liturgical year; then, when they are used at funerals, both the text and the tune will be familiar to the people. Keep in mind that this is not going to happen overnight. Don't say, "Oh, we can't do that at our parish." Say instead, "Oh, we can't do that at our parish, YET."

To the Musician

By now most of you should have experience with the *Order of Christian Funerals*. But two questions that came up when the rite was brand new still apply: "How will the new funeral Mass be different from the previous one?" and "What are the changes?" People were looking for "quick fixes." You know what I mean. Easy answers such as, "The Easter candle should be in its place when we begin and no longer carried in the procession," or "Now we're supposed to put some Christian symbols on the coffin at the beginning of the service," or "We don't incense the body at the gifts time anymore." But the question "What are the changes?" is much more prophetic. Our entire outlook on Christian death and burial will be shaped by this new ritual book. With these rites we will begin to shape the next generation and its approach to Christian death and burial.

A few suggestions to musicians about Christian funerals:

1) The Paschal Mystery includes suffering, death, and resurrection. Music must deal with all of these aspects of the Paschal Mystery at funerals.

2) Use of the psalms is strongly encouraged. They are the way that Jesus prayed.

3) Sentimentality and nostalgia should not be confused with gentleness.

4) There should be a balance in musical style between sounds that are reflective and sounds that call us out of ourselves.

5) Ordinarily, catechesis should take place throughout the liturgical year, not at the time of bereavement.

6) Study the rites. Music should express the action of the rites.

7) Be patient, be prophetic, and teach the children well.

We will be into the twenty-first century before this rite becomes traditional and familiar. But we must begin now. We have been given a very rich and beautiful ritual that we can be proud to pass on to our children.

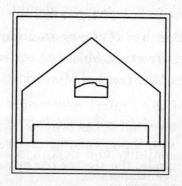

Sacramentals

Book of Blessings

Blessings are part of the church's liturgical life. The *Book of Blessings* (formerly known as the Roman Ritual) has been reassembled and revised since Vatican II. It is *the* official English text for all the major blessings of the church.

The General Introduction from the *Book of Blessings* (#9) states: "As the Church, through the working of the Holy Spirit, fulfills its many-sided ministry of sanctifying, it has accordingly established many forms of blessing. Through them it calls us to praise God, encourages us to implore [God's] protection, exhorts us to seek [God's] mercy by our holiness of life, and provides us with ways of praying that God will grant the favors we ask."

The typical celebration of a blessing consists of two parts: first, the proclamation of the word of God, and second, the praise of God's goodness and the petition for God's help (#20). The proclamation of the word may include several readings, a psalm, a period of prayerful silence, even a short homily, if desired. The centerpiece of the second part of the celebration is the blessing formulary itself, along with the accompanying proper outward sign. Intercessions may be said before or after. Outward accompanying signs commonly used are: the outstretching, raising, or joining of the hands; the laying on of hands; the sign of the cross; sprinkling with holy water; and incensation.

Does all of this sound foreign to you? Well, it's not all new. We've been doing it for years. It's just that now it's all together in a book. You may be familiar with the blessing of a new organ, a new building, blessings before and after meals, for a baptismal font, religious articles, the blessing of throats, ashes, advent wreath, and liturgical ministers. Some other things, however, may be new to you, such as blessings for the welcoming and departure of parishioners, the blessing of mothers on Mother's day and fathers on Father's day, fields and flocks, boats and fishing gear, athletic events, teachers, students, and Christmas trees.

The book is divided into six major sections and two appendices. Part I (Chapters 1-9) consists of "Blessings Directly Pertaining to Persons." These include some very fine celebrational texts including a Blessing of Parents and an Adopted Child, of an Engaged Couple, of Sons and Daughters, of the Sick, and of a Victim of Crime or Oppression.

Part II (Chapters 10-30, with an introduction) contains "Blessings Related to Buildings and to Various Forms of Human Activity."

Part III (Chapters 31-43, with an introduction) contains "Blessings of Objects that Are Designed or Erected for Use in Churches, Either in the Liturgy or in Popular Devotions." (Some title, huh?) You are probably familiar with many of these.

Part IV (Chapters 44-46, with an introduction) contains "Blessings of Articles Meant to Foster the Devotion of the Christian People." Rosaries, scapulars, etc., are accounted for here.

Part V (Chapters 47-59, with an introduction) contains "Blessings Related to Feasts and Seasons."

Part VI (Chapters 60-71, with an introduction) contains "Blessings for Various Needs and Occasions" and it covers a multitude of them.

Take particular note of Appendix II, which contains Solemn Blessings and Prayers over the People. These are very useful.

How to Bless — Who to Bless

Here are some suggestions for the blessing of ministers during the liturgy.

When we commission catechetical or liturgical ministers, for example, try having them rise in their places but not come forward. Why do we so often bring people to the "sanctuary" for commissioning or blessing? Maybe the answer is, "But we've always done it that way." Why not just let them stand in place as the presider and other members of the assembly extend arms to pray over them? Everyone finds this an empowering moment for ministry. Might even members of the assembly grasp more fully their own priestly ministry in Christ through this action?

On Youth Sunday in some parishes, young people read, usher, minister at the altar, lead song, or minister eucharist for the liturgical celebration. This practice has advantages: youth involvement and visibility. But do we receive some inappropriate unspoken messages here? What about those teens — the young and the restless in the pews — who are not interested or gifted in liturgical ministries? It's not for everyone, you know.

To be better Christians, do we have to minister in a more specialized way than do other members of the liturgical assembly? Should we perpetuate the view that to participate

185

well, we need to serve in a liturgical ministry in the church beyond that of the assembly member? Does worshiping no longer suffice? Should we keep giving a signal to young and old and to the next generation that the ministry of the liturgical assembly ranks lower than a more specialized ministry? Wouldn't it be better to ask all teenagers to stand in their places on the particular Sunday so that we may pray over them? Again, the assembly members, along with the presider, would extend arms over them in priestly blessing with Christ. When we see parents pray over their children — or children over their parents — are we not moved? This may take place at all Masses that day. Such affirmation offers two experiences: membership in the community of faith and participation in Christ's priesthood for all baptized persons, young and old.

A Final Thought . . .

Let It Be

Mary said "yes" to something she did not understand. She could have said "no," but she knew that there was a "rightness" about her obedient response. As a result, salvation history has been shaped. You may be serving and struggling alone in your parish, but you are also part of a great family (and we *are* family) of liturgical ministers across the country. Through my encounters with many of you, in person or by mail, I have become very aware of some common traits you possess with one another: 1) You are constantly struggling because you have said "yes" to your particular community; 2) You are the movers and shapers of the spirituality of the parish; and 3) You have a sense of "rightness" about your "call to serve" though you may not fully understand why you have been called.

The waters may seem uncharted, the journey long, and the financial rewards? The military has a term . . . we ought to get "combat pay." Who knows just how important your continued "yes" may be? Stay with it. We need you and we need one another.

Bibliography

Here are some suggestions for basic liturgical reading.

The Basics

The introductions to the *Sacramentary* and the *Lectionary* (included in *The Liturgy Documents*).

General Instruction of the Roman Missal (available from United States Catholic Conference, also included in *The Liturgy Documents*).

Directory for Masses with Children (found in the introductory material in the front of the Sacramentary. Also included in *The Liturgy Documents).*

Music in Catholic Worship (United States Catholic Conference; also included in *The Liturgy Documents*).

Liturgical Music Today (U.S. Catholic Conference. Also included in *The Liturgy Documents).*

The Mystery of Faith: A Study of the Structural Elements of the Order of Mass (Washington, DC: FDLC, 1981).

The Liturgy Documents: A Parish Resource, third edition, (Chicago: Liturgy Training Publications, 1991).

The Rites of the Catholic Church (New York: Pueblo).

Environment and Art in Catholic Worship (Washington, DC: United States Catholic Conference, also included in *The Liturgy Documents*).

Constitution on the Sacred Liturgy (see *The Liturgy Documents*).

Invaluable Reference Works

The New Dictionary of Sacramental Worship, Peter Fink, SJ, editor (Collegeville, MN: Liturgical Press, 1990).

The New Dictionary of Theology , Joseph A. Komonchak, Mary Collins, Dermot A. Lane, editors (Collegeville, MN: Liturgical Press, 1987).

Helpful Resources

Celebrating Marriage: Preparing the Wedding Liturgy, Paul Covino, editor (Washington, DC: Pastoral Press, 1987).

Celebration: Theology, Ministry And Practice, Eugene Walsh (Portland, OR: Oregon Catholic Press, 1994) edition #9853

Giving Life: Ministry Of The Parish Sunday Assembly – Assembly Edition, Eugene Walsh (Portland, OR: Oregon Catholic Press, 1993) edition #9871

Giving Life: Ministry Of The Parish Sunday Assembly – Leader's Guide, Eugene Walsh (Portland, OR: Oregon Catholic Press, 1993) edition #9854

Gladness Their Escort, Monika Hellwig (Collegeville, MN: Liturgical Press, 1988).

The Ministry of Music (second edition), William Bauman, edited by Elaine Rendler and Tom Fuller (Washington, DC: Liturgical Conference, 1979).

Liturgy Committee Basics: A No-Nonsense Guide, Thomas Baker and Frank Ferrone (Washington, DC: Pastoral Press, 1985).

Liturgy Made Simple, Mark Searle (Collegeville, MN: Liturgical Press, 1981).

Parish Celebrations: A Reflective Guide for Liturgy Planning, Dennis Geaney and Dolly Sokol (Mystic, CT: Twenty-Third Publications, 1983).

Preparing for Liturgy: A Theology and Spirituality, Austin Fleming (Washington, DC: Pastoral Press, 1985).

Proclaiming God's Love In Song, Eugene Walsh (Portland, OR: Oregon Catholic Press, 1994) edition #9856

Proclaiming God's Love In Word And Deed, Eugene Walsh (Portland, OR: Oregon Catholic Press, 1994) edition #9855

Spirituality: Christian Life In The World Today, Eugene Walsh (Portland, OR: Oregon Catholic Press, 1993) edition #9844

Still Proclaiming Your Wonders, Walter J. Burghardt, SJ (Mahwah, NJ: Paulist Press, 1984).

The New Jerusalem Bible (New York City, NY: Doubleday, 1985)

To Give Thanks and Praise, Ralph Keifer (Washington, DC: Pastoral Press, 1993).

To Hear and Proclaim, Ralph Keifer (Washington, DC: Pastoral Press, 1993).

Toward An Adult Faith: Talking About The Big Questions, Eugene Walsh (Portland, OR: Oregon Catholic Press, 1994) edition #9857

Walking on Water: Reflections on Faith and Art, Madeleine L'Engle (Wheaton, IL: Harold Shaw Publishers, 1980).

Why Catholics Can't Sing: The Culture of Catholicism and the Triumph of Bad Taste, Thomas Day (New York: Crossroad, 1990).

The Word and Eucharist Handbook, Lawrence Johnson (Resource Publications, 1986).

Yours Is a Share, Austin Fleming (Washington, DC: Pastoral Press, 1985).

Helpful Audio Resources

General Principles for Planning Children's Liturgies, Elaine Rendler (Portland, OR: Oregon Catholic Press 1994) stereo cassette #9913

Liturgy of the Word with Children, Jack Miffleton (Portland, OR: Oregon Catholic Press 1994) stereo cassette #9954

Music for Children's Liturgies, Christopher Walker (Portland, OR: Oregon Catholic Press 1994) stereo cassette #9912

Topical Index